MIN
ZEN
HABITS

Marc Reklau is a Coach, Speaker, and author of seven books including the #1 Amazon Bestseller, *30 Days: Change Your Habits, Change Your Life*, which since April 2015 has been sold and downloaded over 180,000 times and has been translated into Spanish, German, Japanese, Thai, Indonesian, Portuguese and Korean. He wrote the book in 2014 after being fired from his job and literally went from jobless to Bestseller (which is actually the title of his second book).

Marc's mission is to empower people to create the life they want and to give them the resources and tools to make it happen. His message is simple: Many people want to change things in their lives, but few are willing to do a simple set of exercises constantly over a period of time. You can plan and create success and happiness in your life by installing habits that support you on the way to your goals.

If you want to work with Marc directly contact him on his homepage www.marcreklau.com where you also find more information about him. You can connect with him on Twitter @MarcReklau, Facebook or on his website www.goodhabitsacademy.com.

Manuel Villa has a degree in Business Administration and a master's in Business Administration from ESADE. He has worked for more than 20 years in communication, specializing in Research and Strategic Planning, reaching positions of high responsibility in several multinational companies. He has been giving talks, courses and initiation to Zen meditation (Soto tradition) retreats for more than 10 years, and he is the introducer of the Mindful zen practice and Mindfulzen Business in Spain, which establishes a solid bridge between East and West, between Mindfulness and Zen. But above all, it should be noted that he is a happy man.

MINDFUL ZEN HABITS

FROM SUFFERING TO HAPPINESS IN
30 DAYS

Marc Reklau & Manuel Villa

RUPA

Published by
Rupa Publications India Pvt. Ltd 2021
7/16, Ansari Road, Daryaganj
New Delhi 110002

Sales Centres:
Allahabad Bengaluru Chennai
Hyderabad Jaipur Kathmandu
Kolkata Mumbai

This English language edition for Indian subcontinent published by
special arrangement with Montse Cortazar Literary Agency
(www.montsecortazar.com)

ISBN: 978-81-291-4490-4

Seventh impression 2022

10 9 8 7

Printed in India

Disclaimer

This book is designed to provide information and motivation to our readers. It is sold with the understanding that the publisher is not engaged to render any type of psychological, legal, or any other kind of professional advice. The instructions and advice in this book are not intended as a substitute for counseling. The content of each chapter is the sole expression and opinion of its author. No warranties or guarantees are expressed or implied by the author's and publisher's choice to include any of the content in this volume. Neither the publisher nor the individual author shall be liable for any physical, psychological, emotional, financial, or commercial damages, including, but not limited to, special, incidental, consequential or other damages. Our views and rights are the same:

You must test everything for yourself according to your own situation talents and aspirations. You are responsible for your own decisions, choices, actions, and results.

Manuel Villa & Marc Reklau

CONTENTS

Prologue by Marc Reklau   *xi*

DAY 1:   Accept That Suffering Is Not Always Optional   1

DAY 2:   Open a Gap: Breathe and Meditate   6

DAY 3:   Let Your Body Speak and Guide You   11

DAY 4:   Stop the Systematic Hurrying   15

DAY 5:   You Have Four Aces and a Joker in Your Hand.
         Now, Play Your Cards   19

DAY 6:   Do Not Lose Your Compass in the Face of the
         Tornado   24

DAY 7:   Attitudes and Beliefs are the Parents of Your
         Mood   27

DAY 8:   Your Values Should Not Be in the Hereafter   32

DAY 9: Undo Your Identification with Your Thoughts 36

DAY 10: Accept Your Emotions   40

DAY 11: Disconnect the Amplifier of Your Beliefs and
        Activate Useful Thinking   44

DAY 12: Temper the Urge to Do More   49

DAY 13: Nourish Your Values   53

DAY 14: Act Accordingly   57

DAY 15: Do Not Settle. Open the Doors to Happiness 61

DAY 16: The Power of Focus   65

DAY 17: Self-Discipline and Commitment   71

DAY 18: Change Your Habits, Change Your Life   75

DAY 19: Be the Change   82

DAY 20: Write Down Your Goals and Achieve Them 87

DAY 21: The Power of Your Words   95

DAY 22: Never Ever Give Up   99

DAY 23: The Most Important Tool   107

DAY 24: Stop Hanging Out with Toxic People   113

DAY 25: Listen to People, Really   120

DAY 26: Spend Time with Your Family   124

DAY 27: Believe It until You Become It   128

DAY 28: Your Best Investment   131

DAY 29: How to Deal with Problems   135

DAY 30: More Happiness Habits   141

Epilogue by Manuel Villa   151

PROLOGUE

By Marc Reklau

This is the best time in history to be alive. Technological progress is amazing. You're practically wearing your office in the pocket of your trousers. Health experts say that thanks to the progress in medicine we will be able to live over a hundred years, and well at that. Even with this news, it seems people are becoming unhappier and unhappier. Depression and suicide rates have multiplied in the past decades, as has the use of anti-depressants. The onset age of depression today is fourteen and a half, when fifty years ago it was 29. Not to mention the divorce rate, which is at a record high of 60 per cent. What is going on?

When Manuel and I first met, we found out we had a lot in common. Manuel, the quiet, balanced creator of the Mindfulzen and Mindfulzen Business techniques, introducing this style that builds a solid bridge between East and West, between mindfulness and zen. And I have been a lifelong student of happiness myself. It seems that all my life I wanted just that—to bring a little bit of happiness into others' lives, to improve their life a bit by being an example that you can be happy no matter what circumstances you come from.

Science is on our side. In the last two decades, there has been a revolution in the field of psychology, and some of the best psychologists found out that happiness is not something that comes from the outside, our external circumstances, but depends much more on our habits, our thoughts, our beliefs and our attitude than we ever thought. Scientifically speaking, we can choose to be happy by choosing where we put our attention. Happiness is an internal state. It's creating simple little habits day in and day out, like setting goals, being grateful, meditating or doing physical exercise.

In this book, you will learn how to be happy here and now with what you have, so you can stop searching for happiness and become aware that if you look really closely, it's everywhere. Once you stop searching, you'll see it was there all along. It's in the small pleasures of life that you ignore while you are searching for the big things.

Naturally, happiness is something very intimate and personal, and everyone has a different definition of it. There is no one-size-fits-all solution. Happiness is what it is to YOU. And that's totally ok. The exercises will still work—regardless of what happiness means for you.

If we want to understand how to become happier, first we have to accept that our time on this planet is limited. We all have a common destination, which we will arrive at sooner or later, and even knowing so, we live our lives as if we had all the time in the world.

So what are the people closest to this destination saying about it? It is probably an excellent idea to listen to them.

Bronnie Ware, an Australian nurse who accompanied the dying and wrote a book about her experiences noted five of their regrets, which is also the title of her book:

1. I wish I had had the courage to live a life true to myself, and not the life others expected of me.
2. I wish I hadn't worked so hard.
3. I wish I had had the courage to express my emotions.
4. I wish I had stayed in contact with my friends.
5. I wish I had allowed myself to be happier.

Do yourself a favor and start living NOW: not after the kids are out of the house, after having finished the next project, after having bought that new car, after having moved to that new home, or after having gotten that raise at work that you've been waiting for forever. Don't be one of these people that 'don't have time' but spend 30 hours per week in front of the TV, playing video games, or partying.

In this book, we want to take you from suffering to happiness. It's simple but it won't be easy. You'll have to arm yourself with a good dose of patience and perseverance, a bit of self-discipline (don't worry, just a little, we promise), a bit of curiosity, and the will to learn something new.

You'll find concepts you won't like at all. Try them before ruling them out. You'll find things that will be so simple that you'll say to yourself, , 'It can't be that simple.' Try them. You might even find things that seem straight-out crazy and think, 'What are those two clowns saying now?' Try them.

In this book the 'this doesn't work for me' excuse doesn't work. Try it, and then evaluate it.

Happiness is not for idiots. It's a combination of habits and methods that you can learn and that will improve your personal as well as professional life. Happy and optimistic workers perform better, earn more, sell more, and they are safer at their workplace—meaning that they are less prone to be let go.

Create your own happiness. Happiness is a choice, and the most significant obstacles are self-created limitations, like believing that you are not worthy of happiness. If you think you don't deserve to be happy, you also believe that you don't deserve the good things in life, the things that satisfy you, and this is precisely what will keep you from being happy, because as long as you hold on to that belief, you will sabotage yourself wherever you can. Don't worry, you can learn to be happier.

Science has proven that happiness is a choice. It depends on what we choose to focus on. Choose happiness. Choose to focus on all the good things that surround you. Smile a lot. Be thankful for what you have in your life. Meditate for five minutes a day. Exercise for 30 minutes three times a week. These are the scientifically proven exercises that will make you happier if you do them over a period of time.

The difference between happy people and unhappy people is not that one group feels sad or depressed and the other doesn't. The difference is that happy people recover more quickly from these painful emotions. Happiness doesn't just happen to you. It's a choice that requires effort.

It's practising little habits like optimism and joy during a period of time.

Don't expect anything or anybody to make you happy—not even Manuel or me—because the wait could be eternal. No person or circumstance can make you happy. Only YOU can make you happy. What we can do is give you the information.

Happiness is inner work. External circumstances are only responsible for 10 per cent of your happiness. The other 90 per cent is how you act when faced with these circumstances and what attitude you choose to adopt. In other words, 'Life is 10 per cent what happens to you and 90 per cent what YOU do with what happens to you.' Scientifically speaking, external circumstances make up 10 per cent of your happiness, your genes make up 50 per cent of your happiness, and 40 per cent of your happiness is made up by intentional activities—and that's where the learning and exercises come into play.

Some people are simply born happier than others. Period. But if you are born a bit unhappier and do the exercises, you'll surely end up happier than a person that was born happier than you but doesn't do the exercises.

What both formulas have in common is how little the external circumstances influence our happiness. Generally, we assume that our external circumstances have a far bigger impact on our lives and on our happiness.

Be happy with who you are. The funny thing is that often you'll find happiness when you stop looking for it. Enjoy every moment of your life. Expect miracles and opportunities around every corner, and sooner or later you'll find them. No matter what you focus on, you'll see more of it. Choose to concentrate on opportunities, choose to focus on the good. Choose to focus on happiness, and you will create it in your life.

Let's do this!

1

ACCEPT THAT SUFFERING IS NOT ALWAYS OPTIONAL (BUT PART AND PARCEL OF LIFE ITSELF)

One of the phrases attributed to Buddha, and widely repeated in social networks, tells us that 'pain is inevitable, while suffering is optional.' Regardless of the credibility we give to that phrase, let's not forget that Buddha passed through this world more than 2500 years ago, and that Buddhism is a tradition of oral transmission. This statement raises several interesting points of debate. What differentiates pain from suffering? Is suffering really optional? Semantics are always as attractive as they are dangerous.

If we understand that pain always carries a physical component and that suffering is something totally mental, we will be contradicting the most modern theories that link mind and body to levels until recently unsuspected, a link also widely intuited and defended by meditation and the practice of Zen for a long time. Therefore it doesn't seem that this line of argument is the most appropriate.

It is perhaps more possible to associate pain with an emotion (physical and chemical), and suffering with an accumulation of thoughts (also physico-chemical) that adhere to it. In this sense, it is clear that allowing ourselves to feel the emotion of pain without added mental tribulation keeps suffering to a minimum. It is as if we could take away the bitterness and anxiety from suffering, like 'milk without lactose.'

In my opinion, Zen meditation is the technique that best supports this last proposal. A thesis that also subscribes to the Acceptance and Commitment Therapy, or ACT. Meditation, dis-identifying with our thoughts and fully accepting our emotions, but without getting caught up in any more reflections as to why, is the best formula I know of to 'skim' off anxiety and keep only the 'dry extract' of the most inevitable pain, more integral to life itself.

We are talking about a worthwhile exercise, because consumer society continually teaches us how to enjoy pleasure to the extreme and beyond, but nobody tells us how to learn to handle frustration or how to deal with suffering. Hence the current 'success' of zen and sitting meditation, because it is positioned right in the middle of that vacuum. The connection that meditation provides is not only the best balm for pain, but it allows you to experience suffering without so much anxiety or added bitterness.

Zen (meditation) does not look the other way, does not elude anything, does not deny anything, does not rationalize excuses, does not suppress feelings. Zen (meditation) confronts us with ourselves, shows us ourselves with using the mirror of others, and like a good teacher, supports us in our responsibility to overcome the circumstances without the need for our behavior to be necessarily exemplary.

The smile of zen is kind, grateful, and flexible, but at the same time firm and secure. There is nothing like this haven of peace to catch your breath. Soft and light, the wind, the breath comforts us in the immensity of its embrace, in the eternity of its validity. But beware, meditation is not just comfort, meditation is a 'rush' of energy manifested as great strength. No need for great fuss, no need for sound recognition, meditation is instituted as the best energetic balm of the moment. If you suffer, meditate, and, although initially it's only for a few moments, everything shall pass.

The 'poison' that clouds genuine suffering is called guilt, arrogance, or denial of our inherent vulnerability. The rest is nothing but healthy 'alarm clocks.' Remember that if you resist, it persists; if you accept, you transform. Pascal said that 'misfortune reveals to the soul lights that prosperity fails to perceive.'

Life is unfair, and Bill Gates himself admits to it. We cannot expect 'the tiger not to scratch us because we are vegetarians,' but no one can take away the satisfaction of being able to face obstacles with serenity and peace, which are comforting in themselves (and don't rule out that 'the tiger' might get infected as well).

The secret lies in not being carried away by inertia, by attitudes and beliefs that we are not even aware of, and which undermine our morale. When we have an open attitude, with our own stimulating and well-established beliefs, our mood cannot be other than the right one. And with a proper state of mind, the values that grow are a stimulus of boundless faith, a faith that moves mountains, a faith that is not mere theoretical abstraction, but clearly consequential behavior.

But to do this, we must not get carried away by emotions and thoughts that we can't control. We must open a gap and realize that we are not omnipotent, but not useless either. It's in our hands to manage the situation: paying attention and strengthening our conviction. From there, suffering is undoubtedly set to lose.

2

OPEN A GAP: BREATHE AND MEDITATE

The most challenging thing is to start. Habits, inertia, haste. They all make us react and respond without paying any attention. We live on autopilot, running after thousands of novelties that do not bring anything new. Constant, accelerated, cumulative, and aggressive change has led us to the most complete alienation. We have the feeling that we are not living, but that we are somehow lived, but we do not know how to break that vicious cycle, with that 'experiential spin,' the 'Samsara' that surrounds us and confuses us.

Many people say that they don't meditate because they

don't have time. They probably have other priorities, right? Ten or twenty minutes a day is not a lot. And if we dedicate that amount of time daily to physical hygiene, all the more reason we should dedicate it to mental health. Nothing happens if we do not meditate for a day or two (it is like going twenty-four or forty-eight hours without showering), but if we do not find space to rest and rediscover ourselves on a regular and daily basis, we will end up being victims of the abuse of the volatile, uncertain, complex and ambiguous (VUCA) world that is apparently tormenting us. And from there it's only one step to blindness, tunnel vision, rigidity, and perpetual bitterness. From 'Run, run, I'll catch you,' we should go to 'Come, I'm waiting for you to give you a hug.' But how? Where do I begin?

My recommendation is that before you start to meditate sitting on the floor, chasing yet another ideal (this time to keep the 'mind blank'!), you just sit comfortably in a chair and devote five or six minutes (no less - no more) to paying attention to your breathing. Conscious breathing without forcing anything. Observe how inspiration and expiration occur. Is it fast? Slow? Have you noticed that there isn't one without the other? There is no inhalation without letting go, nor vice versa.

Observe, feel the union of the opposites, do not judge,

do not interpret, do not search for a reason or try to correct anything. Without interference, if you pay full attention, you will go from observation (to conclude something) to contemplation (out of pure curiosity) without any effort. Going from observing to contemplating is something wonderful. It is to transcend the ego, to stop giving everything a practical, instrumental sense, and to be able to see ourselves in perspective, taking a kind distance to visualize ourselves again - this time from empathy and compassion. As I said, something wonderful. Observing to improve immediately? No, contemplating for the pleasure of contemplating. If appropriate, everything will progress without further intervention of will and inquisitorial effort. Pressure is what prevents evolution.

When this exercise has already hooked us, and we have practiced it for at least a week, we can go look for a quiet corner in which to meditate. It can be on the terrace, in the bedroom or in the living room; the important thing is that to begin with, it should be an airy space, quiet and more or less silent at the time we are going to practice. It does not matter if we meditate in the morning or at night, but it is important to make it a habit and, consequently, it is good to do it at the same time every day.

It is simply a matter of sitting down with a straight back

relaxed shoulders (if possible, without leaning against the backrest), hands resting on the thighs, feet firmly anchored to the ground, and absolute stillness. In the beginning, stability is almost more important than posture. Silence and stillness will be our great teachers.

Silence teaches us that the constant whispers of thought are only vain fleeting ideas that we can receive and abandon affectionately, in order to concentrate again on the joy of conscious breathing.

The stillness—remaining motionless against any temptation of activity or postural 'correction,' because of itching, discomfort or even pain, teaches us the 'impermanence' of sensations and the naturalness with which emotions circulate.

Breathing consciously and meditating patiently is the best training to later 'open a gap' and neither react viscerally nor respond falsely. Breathing and meditating, observing and contemplating, attention and concentration, silence and stillness—all united to reconnect with what matters most: our most authentic self, our most human condition, life in the present.

Meditating is not relaxing, it's calming down, although all the turbulences, conflicts and repressions that we have swept under the rug of hurry and hyperactivity spontaneously reappear. That's why the comments 'Meditation does not relax me,' or 'I get even more nervous when I meditate,' don't count. When they come up, I'm tempted to respond, 'That's what it's about, letting go, letting go of the nervousness and anxiety, that tension, that voraciousness for solving, to be able to embrace the calm that can appease them, take them on, and, ultimately overcome them.' Sport can help us, but it's meditation that will allow us to build a solid base so that we do not fall into a new forward flight. Remember: what we avoid grows, and only what we accept is transformed.

Following this line of thought, it is not surprising that, as we said, initially instead of relaxation, new or unknown tensions arise, both mental and physical, and that it is the discomfort of the body that first warns us that the process of 'healing' is occurring. It follows that after the exercises of conscious breathing, it is convenient to listen to the body.

3

LET YOUR BODY SPEAK AND GUIDE YOU

The body, that great forgotten element. Yes, forgotten: even those of us who take care of our body and exercise it with prudent doses of exercise forget that our body must be loved. We use it as we please, day and night at our orders and for our interests. 'Now lose weight, now stretch yourself, now try your best, now do not rest, now do not stop, now eat all the candy, now ...'

How long has it been since you last looked at your hands, feet, or knees, and thanked them for everything they 'do for you'? This is not a joke. Hug yourself for a minute. Thank your body for everything it 'does for you.'

Now let's focus on the energies, often opposed to one another, that manifest in our body in the form of somatizations, cramps, or general tensions. We will now listen to our body not only to know what is happening to us but also to try to recognize what it is asking of us.

How does your body feel right now? Read the text that we propose below, and then stand up and ask yourself: Can you define in a single word how you feel your body right now? What is\the predominant feeling? Can you locate it anywhere in particular? On which part of your body?

Close your eyes. Stop controlling. Connect with your inner self. Practice conscious breathing. Let your body speak quietly and guide you.

What is your level of vitality? From your body, or perhaps from your heart, can you connect with the wounds that you have lived experienced most recently? Let yourself be cradled by the beating of your heart. Pay attention, listen to the timid rumble of your pulse. If you are completely silent, you will clearly perceive it. Let your heart recover its natural cardiac coherence and stay in suspense listening to it. Breathing and heartbeat are synchronized almost without our noticing.

Bring your attention once again towards the tensest or blocked area. Feel the weight it bears. Note the tingling that occurs in that area by paying special attention. Stay there, let the attention do its work for a few minutes. Smile. Thank the body for its enormous wisdom. Thank it for what it's undoubtedly telling you, explaining to you, or even warning you of.

Open your eyes very slowly. Wake up to the here and now.

This quick little check of consciousness is essential not only to recognize the first symptoms that should lead us to the doctor, but also to show the intimate link between emotion, tension and somatization. As long as the meditative practice does not work this aspect spontaneously, it is good to do this exercise separately.

The body is not just a vehicle, it is not only a mere instrument that we can serve at our whim, but it is a gift that deserves gratitude. Being grateful to our body: caring for it and loving it without falling into hard asceticisms or hedonistic excesses, is the first step towards happiness, since, as we will see two chapters later, gratitude sets in motion a whole virtuous process that is opposed to the vicious cycle of urgency and hyperactivity that we mentioned before.

Do not mistreat yourself. As Carl Jung said, vices and addictions are nothing more than the most habitual substitutes for suffering. Thanks to the process that we are undertaking, we have learned that suffering should not be hidden or avoided, but brought to the surface and assumed as an inherent part of life itself. This should help us understand that any escape route confuses us more than it clarifies, and everything starts in the body.

If you love yourself, you nourish yourself well, you exercise well, and you take good care of yourself. Food, sports, hygiene, and care should not be linked to fashions, appearances, and immediate pleasure, but to the awareness that the body we occupy is our home and deserves, at the very least, not to be systematically punished by our false pastime distractions predetermined by consumer society. What's more, nutrition, rest, and exercise are the three pillars of our energy. And without energy, there is no passion, there is no vitality. Wanting to build on weakness—physical, emotional or mental—is to build on an unstable foundation.

4

STOP THE SYSTEMATIC HURRYING

Don't hurry! Easy to say. Difficult to put in action. When we broach this topic in company courses and seminars, people laugh. 'How are we going to slow down if we're already not getting there at the current speed?' The question is: where do we get to? Or better yet: At what price?

We all know that success and happiness are not destinations but a path. So we had better be attentive to where we step, right?

It is not about letting the body burn out if it's already burning, but to stop running continuously. I challenge you to be aware of the times you walk in a hurry for no apparent reason. Why run constantly? If we usually run, it's because we're definitely running away from something. Let what has to emerge emerge. A conscious present is the best gift.

Slowing down our our pace of life will not only affect our health positively, but it will become a habit of effectiveness.

In today's society, we systematically sacrifice efficacy for efficiency, and quality for quantity. And we already know that greater efficiency in going after a mistaken goal is the worst of errors. The clarity of our goals requires us to contemplate the horizon regularly, today more than ever, and that is not achieved without giving up running around senselessly.

Take it easy, truth is not in a hurry. Just like that forgotten paper at the bottom of the pile has lost its validity without anyone being alarmed, meditation allows false urgencies to be diluted in a calm and creative rest in the here and now. Invite yourself to a coffee with yourself. Without thinking about anything concrete. Not wandering, but making a pilgrimage to the re-encounter with fullness.

Keep in mind that slowing down does not mean postponing, much less procrastinating, but rather deciding: acting by our particular criteria (without inherited automatisms) or diluting the pressure to 'do something' hastily and without any real meaning for the moment.

Consciously slowing down our pace of life has at least three obvious advantages:

It allows us to listen more and interrupt less.

It opens a space for us to know and know ourselves better.

It allows us to discover the magic of empathy with others.

In our relationships, whether personal, professional, or of any kind, slowing down takes the form of learning to listen actively. And the person who listens always learns more than the person who doesn't stop talking. Listening is silencing the ego. Tasting the silences, the other person's words with attention is the best sign that something is changing inside of us. Infinite advantages. Try and see. Just for a day, stop saving, judging, complaining and criticizing, and the change of attitude will become a fact.

Parallel to this change, you will notice that you tune in better to the gift of opportunity. You will know better when and how you should focus on things. According to experts in Behavioral Cognitive Therapy, in more than 90% of cases, we rush into unnecessary worry or premature response. Let's not anticipate events. Let time tell. Let the sky clear up a bit and look for some crack of blue sky before stating that everything is black clouds. Tuning into the present is recovering the joy of living. Do not run or pursue. Take advantage of the energy of the moment. Mature and let mature.

As there are no two without three, all this will result in greater empathy with others (what Buddhists call 'compassion'). Empathy simply generates good vibrations and is the best medicine for a change of attitude. Applied to ourselves, it relieves us of idealized perfectionism. Applied to our neighbor, it vaccinates us against arrogance. Empathy allows us to transcend the ego.

'Take it easy' the Anglo-Saxons tout, and their phrase is not trivial. Although it seems paradoxical, to break with systematic hurry to the point of falling into 'creative boredom' every now and then is the most productive habit that I know. But for this, we must beat 'Ali Baba and his forty (energy) thieves.' The excuses we have come up with to justify the 'junk moments' in front of the television, social networks, WhatsApp or the tabloid press have to be abolished. No more excuses, no more 'It just relaxes me.' If that really relaxes you, your tension must be unbelievably chronic. Check the causes, and do not become addicted to bad solutions. Stop playing cat and mouse with yourself.

5

YOU HAVE FOUR ACES AND A JOKER IN YOUR HAND. NOW, PLAY YOUR CARDS

We all come to this world with four aces in our hands. Gratitude, kindness, acceptance, and authenticity are the sum of four interlinked successes to which we all have access. What's more, it has been proven that there is a domino effect among them, with the repercussion being the fact that the net satisfaction is greater than the sum of the parts. So let's start at the beginning.

If there is a point of departure for this whole process of transformation and change, it's none other than gratitude.

As we know from positive psychology, gratitude is 'the bomb.' Well, the expression is mine, but the content belongs to Martin E.P. Seligman, who confirms that: 'Gratitude is good for you, it's good for others, and the best thing is that it's free!' The systematic practice of gratitude becomes one of the most typical habits of Mindful zen. Maybe at the beginning you might have to force your smile a little, but the effort is worth it because in these matters physics and chemistry are intimately tied to one another. The order of the factors does not alter the product. It does not matter if you first learn to be more grateful and then consistently smile, or if you begin with smiling, although it is at first somewhat fake, and then appreciate the satisfaction that this change of attitude has given you.

From gratitude to kindness there is only one step. It is easy. If one is grateful for what one has, it is natural for him to be kind to another who shares his peace and happiness, even if the interlocutor is not necessarily a participant or direct cause of his satisfaction. It is clear that he who is well with himself is well with others. Kindness opens unsuspected doors. Unruly, petulant or even perverse people end up surrendering to those who do not cease in their kindness.

In the beginning, there may be a certain rebound

effect, but if the 'siege' is persistent, the resistances end up yielding. And what is valid with others is valid for ourselves. If we are more friendly with our mistakes we can correct them better, learn from them instead of escaping from them, avoiding the circumstances that would favor practicing our skills in the face of these challenges, denying the existence of such weaknesses, rationalizing excuses or repressing behaviors.

But not everything should be 'heating pads.' Authenticity is always a banner for lasting changes. Authenticity is not, however, synonymous with the classic 'that's just the way I am,' which is rather indicative of the most absurd rigidity. Authenticity without awareness or flexibility is simply misunderstood self-esteem, or flagrant selfishness, which are essientially the same. Being authentic implies knowing oneself well, knowing one's strengths and weaknesses, nurturing the former, and tempering or recycling the latter in favor of humility and the search for support.

Only then will we be genuinely authentic protagonists of our lives, being aware that everything changes and that everything must change to flow with the times. As we will see later, everything is summarized in solid convictions and flexible approaches. The self that knows that it fully participates in the context in which it lives and develops has many more possibilities of growth. And most importantly, to enjoy that growth, since, as we know, it is the journey and not the destination that is relevant.

Before we finish, let's not forget one last ace, an essential resource: acceptance. Without accepting that not everything is in our hands, the omnipotence sold as 'empowerment' by many of the current self-help books can sabotage our deepest beliefs. Faith, a conviction in our values and principles, is not at odds with the acceptance that as individual beings our nature is inherently vulnerable and perishable.

Taking full responsibility for what concerns us and accepting what does not belong to us prevents the breakdown. Knowing how fragile we are makes us stronger. Distinguishing small setbacks from obstacles, adversities, or even particular dramas will allow us to face the occasional tragedies that may happen to us or happen to our loved ones with greater strength. Raising the level of our pain threshold makes us less 'whiny' and wiser. Lowering our threshold of satisfaction makes us happier and more empathetic. But above all, it is necessary to know how to distinguish the approachable from the inevitable to better manage our energies.

And if all this were not enough, we still have the joker.

Four aces and a winning joker, what more can we ask for? Can you guess what that magic wild card that covers any margin of error in the practice of the four mentioned virtues is? Surely you know. Think about it. It is easy.

Indeed, it can be no other than love. Love solves everything, it is like the universal remedy for any deviation, mistake or failure. And beware, the use of love is no 'botched job' or quick fix, because, as happens with the Japanese art of wabi sabi, it is precisely the arrangement, the union, the patch that gives the piece more added value.

And speaking of values: what good are values? Are they just the moral corsets of an era? Do not skip the next three chapters. You might find an answer to these concerns there.

6

DO NOT LOSE YOUR COMPASS
IN THE FACE OF THE TORNADO

The paradigm change that the Mindful zen technique proposes is straightforward. Instead of letting ourselves be dazzled by theoretical ideals that degenerate into inherited and limiting beliefs and rigid and dogmatic attitudes, the idea is to put all the focus and energy in attention to the present, or Mindfulness.

Let Mindfulness do its job. Do not interfere. Putting our attention in the here and now will undoubtedly lead us to a greater awareness of what is happening, to question our beliefs until we realize that they are nothing more than mental constructions, our own or given to us by others, but since we are already 'inventing', it is better to bet on those that empower our strengths and talents. From there we can move on to healthier values that are closer to the universal principles of humanity, which is not a big distance.

Only three steps: RESET attitudes, REARM beliefs and REACT for a greater commitment to the present.

Attitudes are what we project into the immediate future. Beliefs are what bind us to the past. And the present is our great opportunity to work with both more wisely. Therefore, all our work is to lighten conservative attitudes and relieve limiting beliefs. If we are aware of it, time, silence and stillness will do the rest.

But it is good not to wait until the last moment to see this whole network. Observing it calmly, quietly, and practicing from serenity is good to be able to face the turbulence with greater ease. In great storms is where great sailors are made, but if beforehand we have not learned to navigate calm waters, the waves of the most adverse circumstances will surely defeat us.

Periodically reviewing our attitudes and beliefs regarding the different areas in which we are operating (family, social, professional, spiritual, etc.) is an unavoidable task if we want to live in the present without major upsets. There are only three simple steps: change of attitudes, change of beliefs and review of commitments; but they will provide us with greater coherence between what we think and what we do, a greater congruence between what we feel and what we show, and most importantly, greater consistency and stability over time.

Meditation helps us in that process: it refines attitudes, smooths out roughness, compassionately embraces beliefs without dogmatism, and frees the mind of obsessive thoughts and labels, unnecessary preoccupations and prejudices, useless suffering and superfluous vanities, absurd perfectionisms and catastrophic pessimism, in short, obsolete selfishness. Quietly. Without disturbing anyone.

If not, selfishness constantly dizzies us with claims of pleasure, power or security, and then, thought only echoes worries, prejudices muddy our attitudes, and the limiting beliefs lead us towards bad habits. Recovering 'sanity' is essential, and to that end we have full attention, or mindfulness (a 'magical' antidote against multitasking stress), the total conviction that we are on the right track (the best pain reliever in the face of anxiety), and the 2500-year-old guarantee that Zen meditation offers us to alleviate the vaguest vital anguish.

7

ATTITUDES AND BELIEFS ARE THE PARENTS OF YOUR MOOD

I f we are going to 'reconfigure' our life, to clean up our habits and improve our mood, as we have seen, we will first have to work on our attitudes and beliefs.

Compared with the change of beliefs, changing attitudes is as simple as 'downloading an application.' The firm purpose of 'opening doors and windows to let in fresh air until the atmosphere is renewed' is enough. For some time, in order to generate a space for change, we will have to listen a lot, ask little and not interrupt anyone under any circumstances.

Changing your beliefs is a bit more complex, comparable

perhaps, following the previous metaphor, to a 'change of operating system.' But let's go step by step.

The four riders of the Apocalypse, in terms of bad attitudes for change, are (in order of importance) idealistic perfectionism, overbearing arrogance, constant doubt, and systematically postponing everything. We all have some of each of them, but it is also true that we all have a 'star saboteur.' Have you ever stopped to think about what yours is? We are going to help you see in which of the following matters you invest the most time in your conversations:

Preaching or lecturing that seems to want to 'save us all,' yet does not propose any active solutions on our part, but rather looks to complain bitterly about the situation at hand?

Destructive criticism and the most biting sarcasm about others to disguise our own incompetence by shrouding it as an 'evil of many' or 'you're worse'?

The repetitive habit that puts everything in intentions, without ever reflecting on real performances? Do you repeat the 'Yes, but...' almost without realizing it, and all the while nodding disbelievingly without any real will to change anything?

Are you a 'professional procrastinator'? Do you always find excuses to postpone everything? Is the search, the infinite 'I am on it,' your most common mantra?

It never fails. Tell me what you talk about, and I'll tell you which negative attitude is your weak point. Once you see what it is, do not forget it. Pay special attention not to fall into it unconsciously. Be patient and persistent. You will notice improvement every day, especially if you notice that:

- Perfectionism forgets that without error there is no innovation, and without innovation, there is no evolution or improvement. 'Done is better than perfect,' as Mark Zuckerberg says, and he knows all about it.

- Arrogance prevents you from enjoying life and become yourself. 'As soon as you start to feel important, you become less creative,' states Mick Jagger.

- Relativism makes doubt grow, which is the main trap that can embitter our lives. It's better to make a mistake than to laugh (with 'the smile of the hanged man,' as it is called in Transactional Analysis) and resign oneself to living one's whole life as a sad spectator and frustrated protagonist.

- Eternal procrastination leads us to lose all options. We lose all our energy in maintaining the 'pending issue' without actually ever knowing if it would have worked had it been approached with full conviction. Yes or no, decide now, but do not let yourself be mistreated by the 'tolerances,' which are nothing more than leaks or 'energy thieves.'

In any case, once we are convinced and set in a more open and positive attitude, we can address the change of beliefs: the move from a limiting belief to a stimulating and empowering one.

The most delicate thing at this point is defining the belief we want to substitute. Many times we confuse beliefs with facts, physical evidence, or, conversely, with aspirational change fables that lack sufficient concreteness and clarity to be instituted as attainable goals for change.

It helps to specify the investigation into the roots of these limiting beliefs: parental mandates from childhood that led us to develop prejudices or dysfunctional complexes, preconceived ideas that always 'hung around' at home, traumas or simple details that marked a particular apprehension to address or to show certain thoughts or emotions, fears or insecurities that began at the dawn of of time, etc. In any case, it is essential to ask sincerely what 'secondary' benefits we still obtain today by maintaining that belief: Why haven't we changed it before now? Along with those 'secondary' benefits to keeping it alive (which undoubtedly there are), what would be the real damage that it is causing us, both now and in the future?How does it affect us and those around us? Is it worth it to continue with it?

If the answer is no, we can address a new stimulating belief that replaces it without losing its definition and precision. Beliefs, like all other long-term mental constructions, live off the reinforcements we provide them with. If we stop feeding a belief interpretations and inferences that support this limiting belief within us, and instead turn our attention to reviewing and strengthening facts, tests, and reflections that support the new stimulating belief, the transformation will become a reality. It will then be enough to nourish the new belief to strengthen it: finding the advantages, activating useful thinking and acting accordingly, establishing specific achievement indicators in the short, medium, and long term. However, that will be the subject that we will consider in later chapters.

8

YOUR VALUES SHOULD NOT BE IN THE HEREAFTER

Our Western culture has systematically linked values to morals and has distanced them more and more from the motivations which, are in fact their natural function. To put it another way, we have turned them more into a passive hope, than into active faith and conviction.

Without adding religions, philosophies, and ideologies, meditation is not a doctrine, or even necessarily a practice of overcoming and improvement. Meditation is an experience, an experience of mental hygiene. And its content, absolutely free of charge, brings us closer to the truth of the present, closer to empathy, connection, and compassion demonstrated by facts.

In Mindful zen, we like to say that if God exists, God is undoubtedly a fact. Without action, there is no human nor divine realization.

If your values are not in the here and now and do not encourage you to live your every day with joy and generosity, change them; they are not worthy. Your values should guide and sustain you. If you can not count on them now, they will become a lie, an empty promise, when you need them. Your values should be your energy providers, especially in critical moments. We need those generators here and now to forgive others, to forgive ourselves, to draw strength from weakness, to enjoy the evanescence of life, to live it fully.

The DNA of our soul is made up of our values—if we lose them, or simply idealize them, if we corner them or actually forget them, we risk making Mindfulness and meditation mere instruments of conformism and conservatism. For Mindful zen, there is no meditation without action, there is no Samadhi without Satori. Everything is one, just like inhalation and exhalation are an inseparable part of breathing. Joy and sadness, courage and fear, anger and calm, fullness and emptiness are all expressions of life.

When we accept this, the action that emerges from meditation can only be a loving, free, grateful, kind, authentic and humble, divine action. It does not require effort, it does not seek recognition, it is pure emotion and universal compassion. In it, the reality that we live and interpret merges with the eternal, infinite and universal truth that connects us with the rest of all living beings; and that is our prize, which is more than enough.

Happiness is here and now. Not in 'the here and now,' as is often said. Not in a philosophical or conceptual space of something we call 'the here and now' but literally 'here and now.' Look for it, feel it, smile, yes that's it, that gesture, that decision, that act that changes everything for a moment. Nothing more and nothing less. A fact, a small spark, a sensitive experience that changes our face, and changes our lives.

Once you have recognized it, you will not forget it, and whenever you feel it, which really is whenever you want, if you share it, you will make this instant a good moment for everyone. You will make people approach you with enthusiasm, with the desire that you 'infect' them with your values and your energy, that you encourage them. Yes, that you encourage them (what a word!) to also make their future dreams a happy present reality.

Stop planning, stop generating expectations, stop shuffling around your hurries, beliefs, and ruminations. Just feel the treasure you have in your hands at this moment. You are changing. You're on the right track. Isn't that happiness? Do not let anyone tell you otherwise. They might—consciously or unconsciously—want to convince you that happiness is something else. Do not believe them. Do not believe us. Believe only in what makes you truly happy. Do not look any further. Think no more.

MINDFUL ZEN HABITS

9

UNDO YOUR IDENTIFICATION WITH YOUR THOUGHTS

I n Buddhism, in Zen, there is a lot of talk of the ego. The ego is undoubtedly spoken of as something different from the Western, Freudian definition, and that possibly confuses more than it helps. I am convinced that many of us would like to understand more clearly what the ego is when we put it next to the self, beyond mere philosophical disquisitions.

In Mindful zen, we prefer to avoid the direct confrontation between the ego and the self in order to establish a continuum of levels of consciousness that go from one to the other without 'either of them getting upset.'

In our opinion, it's not that the ego is better or worse than the self; they are merely different, different levels of consciousness.

To perceive these different levels of consciousness one must first disidentify oneself from one's own thoughts, because, just as the fish is not aware that it is not underwater until it comes out of it, we are not aware of our ego until we distance ourselves from it.

Once we are situated with more perspective and in a contemplative mode, it is easy to see the richness that lies in knowing how to harmonically combine as many levels as possible. There are no musical notes better than others, only happier and more pleasant chords.

An individual person holds tastes, interests, beliefs, values, and principles within a single entity. One person contemplates these different levels of consciousness simultaneously. Sometimes they will put all their attention and energy into their tastes and preferences, in other cases they may defend their beliefs with earnestness, but being aware that all those levels are nothing more than 'strings of the same guitar' is enough. That awareness will lead you without even thinking about it to abandon automatisms and be interested in working on the less apparent levels.

To the point that, as if unintentionally, 'scratching,

scratching' (meditating, meditating) one day you discover that 'deep down' we are all the same, we all have a loving base, a blue sky that connects us and resembles us. (Hence the mirror neurons?)

In the Mindful zen retreats that we organize periodically, we do a visual contact exercise in pairs that occasionally allows us to see this fact. The experience is unforgettable, but would we like to stay in that paradise? For the moment, no. We want to return to the present, with its difficulties, its setbacks, our particular interests, and our different preferences. Everything has its moment, but regularly meditating and flying over our different levels of consciousness is something incredible. It provides peace and tranquility that will be reflected in our stability and behavior.

Stop thinking that you are who you think you are. You are that and a lot more. Do not forget the background. Disidentify from your thoughts, delve into your feelings, dive in to meet the essence of the human condition. You will never forget 'those corals,' 'those other fish,' that like you 'already swim without having to put away their clothes.'

Don't think about it too much. Ruminations only make the water muddy. Let the lake of your consciousness relax, let the mud settle, and you will see everything clearly.

Meditate, and you will see yourself clearly reflected in others' eyes, and your thoughts will be translated into compassionate and complicit smiles.

10

ACCEPT YOUR EMOTIONS

Disidentifying yourself from your thoughts does not mean that you forget your emotions—quite the contrary. Generously allow them to have their space. Feel them in deeply. Although they are linked to suffering, they deserve to be taken care of, loved, embraced and cradled by meditation.

Consumer society has been responsible for making us believe that only pleasure and pleasant emotions are welcome. It has invested a lot of money in it, obviously to link these emotions or sensations to their products or services. But desire and pleasure are intimately linked to ambition, and ambition to dissatisfaction. When we get what we want, we already begin to desire whatever is next, and to fear losing what has been achieved in a never-ending race. As an alternative to pleasure with results, Mindful zen is committed to the enjoyment of the process. As we will see later, this is the primary source of happiness. We do not despise pleasure from time to time when it presents itself, but we also do not lose our minds trying to achieve something that entails a painful path with no other incentive than reaching the goal.

In any case, as we said, pleasure and enjoyment are easy to accept, but what happens when they come with negative side effects, and the emotions that we have to experience are negative or unpleasant?

We have become accustomed to avoiding them, to denying them. Moreover, many self-help books advocate 'looking the other way,' 'thinking positive,' and 'making it look like nothing is happening.' We don't believe that that is the solution. Drowning emotions in the unconscious does not seem like a good idea. Emotions have to be experienced, whatever they may be. The worst thing we can do is to cover them up, deny them, reason through them, wallow in them, or suppress them. When we face them, fear disappears, and just as we said that suffering without anxiety acquires other nuances and values, the unpleasant emotion without the wrapping of fear loses its poison.

The risk is therefore to add arguments, reasons, and ruminations that make this emotion something substantial, permanent, particular, and/or radical. When you feel an unpleasant feeling, do not let anyone insist on rationally delving into it, do not let anyone question you and ask you why you feel how you feel, if you have 'no reason be like this.' What do they know?!

Conversely, I invite you to spend some time alone with the emotion. Make friends with your emotion. And if you have the impression that it is an emotion that visits you regularly, smile with enthusiasm. Did you know that a sense of humor is the best transformer of cortisol (which is connected to resilience) into serotonin (which is connected to happiness)? Use it, it's natural, and its side effects are equally beneficial. When your good friend 'the tragic reason that surrounds such a dramatic emotion,' shows up, welcome her by singing, for example: 'My desperate Angelina is here again.' Smile at her, she does not bite. She's just a thought. Let the emotion undress and hug her with all your love, so that she 'does not catch a cold.'

If it's time for sadness, be sad. Sadness helps us to deal with grief.

If it's time to be mad, be mad, but without becoming a slave to it. Rage is useful to set limits and get out of the impasse or rut. And if it's time to cry, cry, as everyone does. When it happens, it happens.

As the Zen saying goes, 'When I eat, I eat. When I sleep, I sleep.'

11

DISCONNECT THE AMPLIFIER
OF YOUR BELIEFS AND
ACTIVATE USEFUL THINKING

One of the most frequently repeated phrases of modern psychology is the one that tells us that the important thing is not what happens to us, but what we do with what happens to us. This is a great truth. If we know how to weather the storm, we will enjoy the calm after the storm even more, and we will be able to face difficulties as they appear (because sooner or later they *will* appear). If we reflect calmly, we will realize that adversities in themselves are not the problem.

What magnifies them and makes us worry prematurely is the automatic connection we establish between adversity and the negative belief that protects it. Limiting beliefs, always on guard, are like radars ready to activate a complete 'neural circuit of worrying' as soon as the slightest excuse is presented. And that radar also has a double functionality: once it has captured a signal, it amplifies it to the maximum in order to extend it to all the emotions and sensations in your body. That's the real problem.

From adversity (Today I overslept, yet again) we go to the belief (I am a disaster), and from there, quickly to the emotion (I am finished, I will never make it), creating a spiral of growing discouragement, pessimism and possible nefarious self-fulfilling prophecies for the immediate future. So how can we break this chain of 'catastrophic' events? What can we do to change the negative neural circuit and connect with a positive spiral that gives us security and prospects of growth?

Four straightforward and very clear guidelines before 'burning all our ships':

- Review if there is evidence, facts, data, or reliable indicators that the adversity might be due to chance or an exception. (To continue with the previous example: 'In ten years of work you can count with the fingers of one hand how many times that I have arrived late to work.')

- Study the different causes—there is never only one—that could have led us to encourage that adversity ('The alarm clock has been without batteries for days now,' 'Lately I'm working late, and I'm going to bed even later,' 'I do not feel especially motivated by what I am doing,' etc.)

- Value the alternative implications that can be taken into account concerning this adversity ('Today I'm going to change the batteries,' 'I am not going to go to bed later than eleven-thirty,' 'This week I'm going to talk to my boss about my need to find new motivations in my work,' etc.)

- And, always, always, utilize useful thinking. Be careful: I didn't say positive or negative thinking, but useful thought in the present moment. ('Will it help me in some way to get to work thinking about the idea that I am a disaster? Will it be good to try to cover up and forget the incident and concentrate on thinking that everything is going smoothly?' No, not at all. So let us now accept useful thought in the here and now: 'This is just a warning, I am not going to worry about this specific incident now, but I am going to deal with this matter this afternoon to make the decisions that I see as appropriate. And the topic doesn't have to go any further.'

This system does not fail. It is not just talk. It works. Put it to the test.

Disidentifying from our thoughts and building only on useful thinking in the here and now are two of the most significant lessons you can find in this book.

Watch the dance of your thoughts as if they were chess pieces. Imagine that the white ones are positive thoughts and the black ones negative thoughts; do not stay with one or the other, you are not playing, after all; it is only your 'monkey mind' that is playing tricks on you.

Look at the board from a distance, and contemplate the strategy of your mind and impose your impartial law: the most healthy and functional thought in the present moment. What does that thought invite you to do? To postpone your ruminations and not to give in to 'hot-headed' reactions?

To decide that you should take action on the matter as soon as possible? To smile and realize that you are overreacting and that it might be better to just forget about it for now, because it really does not matter so much? Let yourself be guided by useful thinking. It never fails. Believe in yourself.

12

TEMPER THE URGE TO DO MORE

A ccording to Behavioral Cognitive Therapy (BCT), in more than 90% of the cases, our worries and negative expectations are not met. We know this. We have an empirical demonstration that this is the case. Moreover, those of us who are expert sufferers know that 99.9% of the time our worrying is in vain. But we 'can't help it,' or we do not know how to. So we'll have to learn.

The anxiety that leads us to take inventory each morning of what will be the most worrying concerns of the day must disappear. We have disconnected the amplifier from our catastrophic beliefs, and we have connected with the peace of the present. We are not going to get ahead of ourselves. We have committed to that. To avoid doing so, we will activate useful thinking in the here and now.

Haste is always a bad counselor. How many times have we worsened the situation because we acted too early? The greed for having 'everything resolved,' 'everything under control,' or 'everything in a glossy, magazine-perfect state' leads to our downfall.

Many of our problems (if not all of them) require a space for maturing, and wanting to speed up solutions not only does not help, but actually harms us, so that once we reach the serene point of useful thinking we do not want to do more. There is nothing more to do. Resting in the wisdom that we have done what we had to do and now all we can do is to wait, is a virtue that is cultivated in meditation.

'No matter how early you rise, the sun won't rise any earlier,' goes the saying, and it is very true. Many times being in a hurry ruins a faster and easier solution. Haste spoils everything, including enjoyment, so of course it will also interfere with the resolution of crises and problems.

Along these lines, Taoism gives us an exciting concept: Wu Wei. Do not interfere. Do not get in the way when 'the die is cast.' We can contemplate with some satisfaction the course of things once we have assumed our responsibilities and we have done what was appropriate. We do not want to spoil it. Shout out 'Wu Wei' to scare away all the alarmist ghosts that want to convince you that if you are not fully aware, fully occupied with that worry, you will fall into disgrace. Shout out 'Wu Wei' and assume that everything will go well, that everything has its process and its moment.

One last note concerning this point: remember that there is nothing more contagious than anxiety. If you demonstrate your true steadiness, you can be criticized, accused, and despised, but in the end (if not before), I guarantee that underneath it all you will be admired.

Those who know how to take life in stride, and problems with serene tranquility, generate a halo of (tremendous) attraction. One gains in self-confidence (although some nerves are still suffering during 'training'), and the rest of the people 'take note' that in the face of adversity, 'it's good to have you near' because your encouragement and advice will be undoubtedly true.

'Stay Calm and Share Comfort,' is the proposal of one of my favorite sayings, and just remembering it, a smile appears on my face. I use it often. I remind myself of it every time I'm going to make a complicated call or write an email that looks like it's going to be a bit hard. And since I started doing so, many people have told me that they have noticed a change, that they are happy to deal with me, that for complicated issues they prefer to talk with me before anyone else in the company. We really do complicate our lives. If you let problems come near you, you will see that they are only challenges, if not great opportunities.

Facing the issues with a 'high' view requires attitude and aptitude, and that's why you are reading this book, isn't it?

13

NOURISH YOUR VALUES

I f you really want to get in shape, and regularly go to the gym and work on a well-established progression program, what is the first thing you do? A check-up, an analysis to know where your strengths and weaknesses are.

If your car is getting older, and it needs oil and some testing to see if it requires new tires, what do we do? We seek advice from a mechanic and get some maintenance done.

So why don't we apply the same criteria to ourselves? Why do we forget to go to any check-up other than the ones dictated by our age and our doctor?

In Mindful zen we have created a mental hygiene check-up (Insight Transformation Venture) that provides us with an easy assessment of attitudes, beliefs, and values, which is focused on decision-making and the development of a plan of action for the short, medium, and long term, in order to walk path of fulfillment, as we will see in the next chapter. You can apply it yourself, and we assure you that the effects won't take long to show up in your daily life.

So far, we have mostly reviewed the first steps toward a change of attitudes and a change of beliefs (for a more detailed account, we would have to go to the book 'The practice of Mindful zen', currently only available in Spanish on Amazon), but we still have something significant to share, something which will be the essential fuel to generate the energy necessary to address all those changes safely: the inspection of the strengths and weaknesses connected to values and principles, an inspection that serves as a guide and supports the entire process.

We think we know what our strengths and weaknesses are, but we don't really. When we do a systematic review of this subject, we find great surprises, especially if we do not limit the check to our own perceptions.

To begin with, it is good to focus on the area that we wish to investigate. Although strengths and weaknesses are usually transversal characteristics of personality that are more or less equally evident in all areas, it is good to begin by studying the particular context that we are most interested in working with (personal, professional, family, motivational, spiritual, etc.). In this specific area, we begin by dissecting our current strengths, our gifts, the natural talents that always accompany us, and that we must cultivate and nurture as if they were our own children. If we do this analysis well, our weaknesses will no doubt also appear alongside, because great virtues inevitably have their associated and proportional Achilles' heels, which must be taken into account so that they do not become insurmountable obstacles.

Once we have mentally 'sketched out' our current profile, with four or five strong points and a similar number of weak points being sufficient, we can go on to project our desired profile, without fantasies or false modesty. The mere contrast will help guide us. From our experience in these matters, we can safely say that many of us carry around an impressive ignorance as to what we want to be like, or at least how we want to be perceived. We have all heard the phrase that: 'If you do not know where you are going, any path will take you' (to your downfall) so, let go of inertia and set the course for your life, but not before knowing what the people that really love you, or even the ones who really know you well but don't necessarily like you, think.

There's nothing more beneficial than informal talks with friends and family, or colleagues, bosses, and subordinates (depending on the area you are working in), to talk about their particular perception of what most characterizes you. There are huge surprises, believe me. If you have never tried it, I guarantee that in more than one case you will be completely amazed.

Knowing what people think of us, if done in an environment of sincere intimacy, is as healthy as the best medical check-up in the world.

It's easy, you just have to set your mind to it, and then do it. Find your qualities, dig into your faults, imagine how you want to be remembered, ask how people see you, ask them to speak with sincerity, without flattery or heated circumstantial criticism. There is no better method to draw the cartography of your life, establish your north and your guiding star, your true values, and being able to nourish them consciously, beginning that very day.

Remember that if you do so, those valuable strengths and those ever endearing weaknesses will accompany you generously in times of difficulty, keeping you on course and illuminating your path. Is that karma? It doesn't make any difference!

14

ACT ACCORDINGLY

Nothing, absolutely nothing of anything you have read to date, in this book, or in any previous or subsequent book, is of any use if you do not take action. In fact, we agree that many of the things you learn in this book are not new. It is necessary to repeat the same truths expressed in one way or another over and over again until we find the key that fits our lock, and the day it 'clicks,' the magic happens.

As Woody Allen says, 'It has taken me more than ten years to change from one day to another.' Well, that's it. Hopefully, everything we're saying here will help you take the plunge. Because the key is the first step, since once you're on the road everything looks different. Everything changes, everything takes on meaning, everything makes sense, the past and the future seem like a constellation, a line of points that suddenly come together in the present acquiring an unsuspected utility, a whole sky of possibilities. That is why we like to talk more about maturity than about learning, because the progression is not linear, but magical: when 'the heavens want, the moon illuminates us with all its clarity,' not a moment before nor after. You just have to be attentive and prepared, or as I would say, available.

Meditation is 'that finger pointing to the moon,' indicating that we are ready. But do not expect anything; things will happen in their due time. It is not about cultivating passive hope, but rather about working on a proactive faith, because we all know that 'If you don't change, nothing will change.' And now we also know where to start (attitude), where to continue (beliefs), what signs along the way will comfort us (state of mind), and what signals will guide us (values and principles). That's great, since it's not just an idea anymore. Now there's a plan, and Let's not forget that motivations must always be concrete.

We need tangible symbols in the short, medium, and long term that will confirm our development and progress. Can you imagine the first scenario in which your so-called change of attitude will be tested? Can you visualize in what situation your change of beliefs will be shown? Can bring to mind a pending issue that will require the strength of values not to lose your nerves? Surely you can. Think of them. Smile, now you have new strength. Let fear accompany you. It is no longer the paralyzing fear of before, it is indicative that you are leaving your comfort zone. 'Keep Calm.'

Without periodic evaluation, there is no progress. Everything that is not taken care of is lost, and what is not measured is forgotten. Set your own indexes for improvement (the Key Performance Index, or KPIs, as they are called in the English-speaking world). They don't need to be sophisticated or rigid assessments. We have seen that tolerance and flexibility are values that are both positive and necessary. Do not be a perfectionist. Be a 'possibilist.' Move forward, make mistakes, fall and get up again. That is constant improvement. That is KAIZEN.

If your confusion is so great that you do not know what parameters to set, we will help you. To start practicing, you do not need to put the horizon too far; on the contrary, the closer, the better. Focus on your day to day, step by step, and ask yourself daily before starting to meditate:

- What 'mistakes' have I acknowledged today? Have I learned anything from them?

- What 'mistakes' have I forgiven others? How have I felt upon not assigning them greater importance?
- What negative temptations have I overcome? or What frustrations have I managed to process without getting mad?
- What have I learned today? What happiness have I been able to share with others?
- What peace has been given to me? And what peace (or good vibrations) have I been able to give?

Make your own list of questions. Don't be shy. Dig deep, where you think you have the greatest need for improvement. Monitor your progression for 30 consecutive days. Make it a habit. Smile at every point, at every slip-up that gives you that little satisfaction of knowing that you are doing well, that you are on the right track.

15

DO NOT SETTLE.
OPEN THE DOORS TO
HAPPINESS

When one has suffered a loss, a drama, or even a tragedy close by, it is hard to recover. Days, weeks, months, even years go by, so that one gets used to living in the shadows. The eyes adapt to living 'in the tunnel,' in low light, and going out and facing the sun hurts. One has already created his own ecosystem and has found a certain sweetness in that dull, sad, and apathetic state. Hence, we need a friend, a companion, a book, a retreat, a reflection, a push, or something otherwise unique that marks a turning point and helps us to wake up.

If we hear that voice that whispers to us that it is time, that everything is over, that compassion has been able to deal with it for the most part, let's not be slow to react. Let's open our eyes, breathe deeply, and let's enjoy life.

Happiness is a choice. Success and happiness are nothing extraordinary. As we have said before, happiness is here and now. You just have to find it and share it. The more you share it, the more it's given away, the more you infect others with it, and the better we all live.

One of the questions we always ask in our training courses is: 'What is success for you?' The answers come quickly, and they all revolve around the idea of achieving a goal. The most primal are concentrated on the most superficial levels of consciousness: money, position, security. The more astute ones point to tranquility, self-realization, inner peace. However, in all of them there is the same hidden trap. Since when is achieving a goal, a goal for which we have had to sacrifice excessively, a success?

Running after the carrot, we have forgotten that we had a tree full of apples on our side. In working for our 'ideals' we have lost our values, and sometimes even our principles. That is why many times tripping over something, real adversity, can be so useful, because it makes us see that in the current race there is no enjoyment, and the prize can't only be in the achievement of the goal.

Success, like happiness, is on the path. It's the journey. Knowing that you are on the right track is the best satisfaction to which we can aspire. Stop to think about it. Feel it in your body. At this very moment you are happy; otherwise, you would not be reading this book.

Either way let's help you some more. Where can we look for the sources of everyday success and happiness? Let me ask you a question:

- How many days have you been programming or improvising a thousand and one tasks for the next 24 hours and you comply with everything without question? Did you reward yourself for it?

- How many doubts and problems have you solved today? How many decisions, more or less important, have you made? Have you congratulated yourself on them? Remember that doubt is one of the main enemies of joy and happiness.

- How many new things have you learned in these last few hours? Isn't it amazing how far you are advancing?

- How many errors have you identified, come to

terms with, and/or corrected? How many have you forgiven? Isn't that excellent news?

And so on indefinitely. Create your own list. Stop inventing complaints, criticism, pain, and suffering, and start a new life full of kisses, hugs, pats on the back, smiles, and winks of real/true complicity.

Life is like this; at every moment it allows us to choose the good side, the compassionate side, the kind, affectionate, grateful, authentic, loving side. Make no mistake. Without vanity, everything is very simple. Meditate. Do not complicate things.

16

THE POWER OF FOCUS

The most important thing on your way to happiness is your focus, or in other words, where you direct your attention. The first step is to retrain your brain to see more of the good things in life.

Many people complain that they don't get what they want out of life without noticing that most of the time they are concentrating on what they *don't* want. The problem is that our brain is structured in a way that you will always see what you focus on. If you need a more mystical approach, just think of the Law of Attraction—you'll attract more of what you focus on. It doesn't matter which path you choose; the important thing is to focus on what you want in your life from now on.

Do you remember when you wanted to buy a particular car, and suddenly you saw it everywhere? Or maybe you had an injured leg or arm, and suddenly your whole town seemed to be limping or with a cast? Do you remember that song that you love (or hate), and suddenly it seems to be played on every radio station?

That's how focus works, and not only for cars, legs, and songs, but also for happiness, success, opportunities, and even sadness, problems, worries, and other painful things. When you search for something, suddenly you see it everywhere. Stavros y Torres said of their research: 'We see what we are looking for and we miss a lot of what we are not looking for, even when it's there. Our experience of the world is influenced by where we direct our attention.'

That's why it's so important to be aware of what you are concentrating on. Are you concentrating on the positive or on the negative? On problems or solutions? On the past or the present?

If you say, 'I'm happy, God am I happy,' and at the same time concentrate mostly on drama, pain, on how bad people treat you, or on how bad the world is, then, my friend, you will see precisely this in your world, even though happiness is also around you. Everything coexists and what makes the difference, what draws it into your reality, is your focus.

And that's something you can learn to control.

Ed Diener describes the power of focus in the following way: 'The way in which we perceive the world is a lot more important for our happiness than objective circumstances. It's not the external that matters, but the internal. It depends on our mood - on what we CHOOSE to concentrate.'

Reread this:

'The way in which we perceive the world is a lot more important for our happiness than objective circumstances. It's not the external that matters, but the internal. It depends on our mood - on what we CHOOSE to concentrate.'

That means that if you concentrate on opportunities, you will see more opportunities. Concentrate on the goodness of people, and you will see good people all around you. Concentrate on success, and success will come your way.

You can use the following questions to change your focus if necessary:

- How can I improve this situation?
- What can I be grateful for in my life?
- What's going really well in my life right now?
- What could I be happy about right now?
- Will this still be important in ten years?
- What is great about this challenge?

- What can I learn from this situation?
- What can I do to improve this situation?

You can change your reality by changing the questions you ask yourself, because these questions will change the way you perceive reality. If you change your focus, and/or if you change your questions, everything is going to change!

Try it! Instead of asking yourself, 'What's not working?' or 'What's going badly?' ask yourself, 'What is going great?,' 'What am doing well?,' 'What are my strengths?,' 'What are my interests?,' or 'What am I good at?,' and you will see it. If you concentrate on what's going well in your life—even if at the moment it's not much—you will see more and more of what's going well. On the other hand, if you only ask, 'What's not working?,' that will be the only thing you see.

So, where is your focus? On what's working? On the positive side of things? Are you in the present? Yes? Great! You are one of those people that makes lemonade out of lemons and finds miracles in the everyday. What a great way to live. We need to respect reality, accept it as it is, and make the best out of everything that happens to us, because sometimes we are not responsible for what happens to us, but we *can* control how we react and how we deal with the things that happen to us.

If you are a person that has always focused on what's not working, on things that don't work out, and on problems, you might be tempted to think that everything I'm saying is stupid, useless crap, that life is not that simple, that who am I to judge you (I'm not judging you, by the way—I've been there), and that for me everything is easy. If so, please keep reading a bit more. If you manage to change your perspective, everything will change. You will have to train a bit, true, but the rewards will be huge. Remember that what I am writing is not metaphysical nonsense, but scientifically proven facts. So bear with us.

Stop thinking that the terrible reality is outside of you, that you are powerless, and that you are a victim of your circumstances. You are not! If you are unhappy at work, just for a moment focus on the good things about it. There is always something. Are your colleagues nice? Are you working close to home? Is the pay-check okay?

And what about your life with your partner or spouse? What good things are there? There must be something going right? If there is nothing there, why are you still with this person? There are seven billion of us on this planet. There will undoubtedly be a partner out there that treats you well.

Learn to accept reality as it is, and then make the best of the situation. Change it if you can. We can all learn to become 'benefit-seekers' by training ourselves to interpret events through the lens of optimism and training our brains to focus on the positive. Remember that 'things don't always happen for the best—but we are capable of making the best of the things that happen to us.'

Many people accept whatever happens to them and then make the best of it. Become one of these people. Remember that everything is temporary and you will be okay again. You lived through other situations, and in the end, everything was fine. This time will be no exception.

If you learn to accept reality as it is and make the best of it, you will reap the benefits that come with this mentality: you'll feel better, you'll be happier in the long term, you'll experience more positive moods, and you'll be less anxious.

So once more: how you perceive the world is a lot more critical to your happiness than circumstances. It's not the outside. It's the inside. It depends on your mind—on your focus.

17

SELF-DISCIPLINE AND COMMITMENT

Being or becoming happy is also a matter of discipline. Happy and discipline? Only a German can write these two words in the same sentence. But I told you. It won't be easy. Happiness is work and effort. It's not something that comes from the outside. It's daily habits that you adopt, and with time, you'll become happier.

Self-discipline will be the foundation of your future happiness, and your road to happiness is deeply connected with your commitment. These character traits will determine whether you do what you said you were going to do, and if you keep on keeping on. They'll keep you on track towards your goals, even when everything seems to be going against you.

Having self-discipline means doing the things you have to do, even if you are not in the mood to do them. If you adopt the habit of doing what is necessary despite not being in the mood for it, your success and happiness are inevitable.

And the best thing of all is that you can train to become self-disciplined, and well, self-discipline is also overrated (I bet you've never heard a German say that).

What? Yes indeed. Self-discipline is overrated. I understand if you are confused now. Me too. Bear with me.

You can train to have more self-discipline and willpower up to a certain point. Self-discipline and willpower are limited, so you can't really depend on them. Throughout the day they run out just as your car runs out of gas, and your cell phone runs out of battery.

So yes, you have a limited quantity of self-discipline, and the question becomes, what you are going to do with it?

Here comes the good news: for your happiness, self-discipline is not essential. Yes, you've read right. For your happiness, self-discipline is not essential. Keep reading.

Have you ever noticed how the vast majority of attempts to change something—organizational or personal—fail? Why is that? Because we depend too much on self-discipline. For example, take your New Year's Resolutions. How are they going?

They say that in 80% of the cases they don't even make it to the end of January. Why? Because they are based on self-discipline.

On the other hand, I suppose that you brush your teeth every day, right? Do you need motivation to do it? Do you need self-discipline to brush your teeth? Do you have to set the goal of 'Tomorrow I will brush my teeth!'? I don't think so. It still works. You are doing it automatically because brushing your teeth is a habit.

So if you shift from depending on self-discipline to achieve change, to introducing new habits, you will need a lot less self-discipline. You might need it the first couple of days when starting a habit, but after that things get a lot easier, and before you know it the habit becomes automatic.

Many times what seems to be discipline (for example, what you can see in the case of athletes) are in reality habits or rituals, and the truth is that habits are the only way to create lasting change.

Transform exercising, not checking your email for three

hours, writing down three things you are grateful for every day, a date night, family dinners, etc., into habits, and write them down in your weekly planner so that they are set in stone. If you don't create rituals or habits, the days, weeks and even years will go by, and you will never do what you wanted to do.

Remember that all of this will not happen in a day. Give yourself some TIME to create habits. How much time? Well, to be honest, all the time you need. Habit experts say that creating a habit takes between 16 and 180 days, 66 days being the average, but the truth is that it depends on the habit and the person. I'm sure you can create easy habits like drinking a glass of lemon water after getting up in the morning in just a couple of days. Getting up at 6 a.m. in the morning to go for a one-hour run might take a lot longer. Does it really matter how long it takes to commit to a better and happier life? It's not that you will ever stop with these good habits if they work, right?

For most habits, 30 days should be enough. The goal is to achieve small successes over and over again. These successes will add up to incredible results with time.

James Clear says that 'habits are the compound interest of self-development.' It couldn't be said better. So go on, build your fortune based on good habits.

18

CHANGE YOUR HABITS, CHANGE YOUR LIFE

L et's talk a bit more about habits. As we mentioned in the last chapter, the only way to create lasting change is by creating habits. We said that it takes between 16 and 180 days to develop a habit, and that even though it depends a lot on both the habit and the person, 30 days is a good benchmark. In any case, don't think too much about how long it takes. That's secondary. The most important thing is to do it over and over again, every day, until you do it automatically. Then the habit has been created.

Aristotle himself said it more than 2500 years ago: we change our lives by changing our habits. By do doing things differently, even small things, we change old behaviors. If we want different results in our lives, we need to do things differently, right? Because as Einstein declared, doing the same things over and over again expecting different results would be madness.

The most important thing about deciding to change your habits is becoming aware of them. Once you are aware of them, equip yourself with that necessary bit of self-discipline and willpower, and the process of change starts. Careful, you'll have to work a bit. I know, you want the quick fix, the magic pill. Sorry, neither of them exist. No false promises here; here we work. One thing: if you work and persist, success is guaranteed. The problem is that many people want to change their lives without making any effort. They want the quick fix, and the quick fix doesn't exist, so they give up. If only they could have patience and work consistently over time on their change, you can be sure they would succeed. Everybody wants to be a champion, until they find out that to become a champion you have to work hard. (If you have found a method for absolute effortless success, please let me know.)

So how do you create new habits? There are various ways. The easiest way to break a bad habit is to substitute it with a good one. For example, you can replace soft drinks with green tea, or your breakfast McMuffin with a banana.

Another way is to introduce the new habit in a ritual that already exists. For example, drinking your freshly pressed green juice after putting on the coffee maker, or going for a run after getting up but before getting into the shower.

Make it as easy as possible; start small and eliminate all the excuses in advance. From personal experience, I'd recommend you try to implement the more difficult habits just after getting up. If you want to introduce a new habit into your life, and don't manage to do so, then analyze why. Which obstacles do you come across? If you want to eat healthier, but always fall back on fast food when you are starving, have cut fruit and veggies prepared—or at least washed in the fridge—so that it will be easier to choose the healthy option.

The key is to put the desired actions or behaviors as close as possible to the path of least resistance. Identify your 'activation energy'—what it is that you need to start, whether it is time, decisions, mental and physical effort, and then reduce them. Make it as easy as possible for you. Shawn Achor explains in his book *The Happiness Advantage*—which, by the way, is one of the best books I have ever read, and has had a profound impact on my life

- that if you can cut the activation energy of habits that lead to success even by as much as 20 seconds, you will be able to reap the benefits in no time.

If you want to smoke less, put your pack of cigarettes as far away as possible, in another room. If you're going to watch less TV, hide the remote, or take out the batteries, and put a book right next to your favorite sofa spot. I have even slept in running clothes (and socks) and had the running shoes right next to the bed so that it's easy to go for a run at 6 a.m.

To get up earlier, I put the alarm clock in another room, and after turning it off, I went straight to the bathroom and brushed my teeth so that I wouldn't go back to bed. It worked!

It might sound ridiculous, but small changes like this can make a huge difference in your life. Try it!

Another trick is to plan what you will do, where, and when. Studies show that people who planned where and when they would exercise exercised over 50% more than those who didn't (all other conditions being equal).

Make rules for yourself. For example: 'I will only check my emails once before noon,' or: 'I will take only one coffee break.'

Some studies confirm that making too many decisions

drain our energy—and we make a lot of decisions every day. With each additional choice that we make, our physical stamina, the ability to perform numerical calculations, the persistence in the face of failure, and our general focus all drastically fall, which in the end results in bad decisions. That's why at the supermarket register we buy things we do not want, or why when we've been shopping all day we start buying things that we do not need at all. That's why you see Mark Zuckerberg or Barack Obama always wearing the same clothes every day—they are eliminating choices in order to make better decisions in critical situations. The more rules you make for yourself or the more you plan out what you will do, the fewer decisions you'll have to make, which will in turn be better ones.

Which bad habits are you going to give up? Being constantly late? Working late? Eating fast food? Procrastinating? Interrupting others while they speak? What else?

And which good habits will you implement? These are some of the habits that many of my clients want to create:

- Exercising three times a week, or walking 10.000 steps a day.
- Concentrating on the positive side of things.

- Writing down three things they are grateful for.
- Working on their goals 15 to 30 minutes every day.
- Going for a morning walk.
- Setting aside 15 minutes of 'me-time' every day.
- Spending more time with family and friends.
- Going meatless a couple of days per week.
- Eating more fruits and vegetables.
- Reading 30 minutes a day.

Don't get overwhelmed. Start with one or two habits at a time, and once you have implemented them, start other ones. Start small. Remember: the path of least resistance. It's better to read one minute a day than to put it off until one week after another it becomes 30 minutes. The same goes for running: walking five minutes a day is better than not walking at all. If you want to change five habits at a time, it might not work because it takes too much energy.

Having a visual interpretation is helpful—a habit tracker, or simply a calendar where you mark every day you made the habit with a cross. Once you see a pattern or many crosses in a row, you won't want to break the chain. If you miss a day, don't worry, just try not miss two in a row if possible. And don't forget to celebrate and reward yourself for your successes and for your progress!

The most important thing is that you DO, that you TAKE ACTION. It should not be no secret that it's also the only way to succeed. The key to creating habits is REPETITION. So put those reps in.

Practice the habit over and over again, until the actions take root in the neuronal chemistry of your brain. Only knowing what you have to do and not doing it is not going to take you anywhere. Everything will stay the same.

So start practicing and go for it!

19

BE THE CHANGE

top trying to change other people. It's impossible.
The ugly truth is that you can't help people that
don't want help. Trying to do so is a waste of time.
Do you know what you *can* do? Be an example. Yes, it's
that simple. Be the change you want to see in the world
(Thank you for this great phrase, Mr. Gandhi). People will
always do as you do, not as you say.

Start seeing other people as your mirrors. The things
that you don't like about them are often things that you
don't like about yourself. They show you what you have to
work on yourself, and/or things that you have to work on
balancing out. It might also be something you are doing
to other people. Does it bother you that somebody keeps

making false promises to you? Who are *you* making false promises to? Are you bothered when your kids tell you that they'll call you in 10 minutes and then don't call you? Who are *you* not calling back?

You are not responsible for other people's behavior. You're only responsible for your own behavior.

When you shift from expecting 'others' (your boss, colleagues, spouse, friends) to change, to 'if I change, then maybe others also change,' the game changes entirely. I repeat: you can't change others. They are the only ones who can change themselves. What you *can* do is accept them as they are, and be the best example and the best person you can be.

Do you complain about your spouse or your co-workers? Be the best spouse or colleague possible. Do you complain about your employees? Be the best boss ever. Do you want to be loved for who you are? Start loving others for who they are. Yes, it really is that simple. Once you become aware of this, everything changes.

And how can you change? Why is changing so difficult? Why are 44% of doctors overweight, despite the fact that they know about the importance of a healthy lifestyle? Why do we all know what we should do, and yet it's still so difficult to do so?

We all know that exercising is good for us, and yet most of us don't exercise regularly. Knowledge alone is not enough; if we don't take action, our knowledge is worthless. 'The man that doesn't read has no advantage over the man that can't read,' said Mark Twain. You can read all the books about the 'Tour de France,' and you still won't be able to win it. You can learn all the cookbooks by heart, but without practice, you still won't be a good cook. It's when you start taking action and start putting you knowledge into practice that you will improve day by day and obtain better results.

Another reason why change is so difficult is that we want to change, but we are not willing to pay the price for it. Everybody wants to be a champion, until they find out that to be a champion you might have to train six hours a day and can't go out partying or just hang around on your couch all day long.

Perhaps you want to lose weight, but you don't want to eat a healthier diet, or maybe you want to exercise, but don't want to get up half an hour earlier. No worries, you'll always find countless excuses.

To find out if you really want to change ask yourself the following questions:

- Do I REALLY want to change?

- Do I want to improve?
- Do I want to change things, character traits, or behaviors that I don't like?

There is yet another obstacle in your way: sometimes you want to change, but subconsciously something is stopping (or sabotaging) you, such as the belief that you don't deserve a better life.

The most important ingredient, and the key to change, is the change of behavior. The only way to achieve lasting change is by introducing an immediate change of behavior, which means doing things differently, doing some of the exercises we learned at the workshop, at the conference, or from the book we are reading, writing down our goals, taking small calculated risks that we haven't taken before, and so on.

If we only listen or read, and don't do anything, we will feel happy and motivated during the workshop or while reading the book. We make big plans and huge goals, only to notice that after a couple of days we go back to our old ways and feel the same emptiness and confusion as before.

A class, a book, or a workshop *can* introduce a change of attitude, but if YOU don't follow up with the according behavioral change, introducing new habits into your life, you'll return to the same place as before. We know that attitude influences our behavior, but our behavior also influences our attitude, and behavior is more powerful. Actions are always more powerful than words.

That's why you can 'fake it until you make it.' You can fake a smile to get a happiness boost. You can 'fake' your posture and body language to get a temporary boost of self-confidence and—if you do it consistently over time—in the long run, more confidence. Your behavior WILL affect your attitude! If you walk with your head held high, looking slightly upwards and straight ahead, there will be chemical changes in your body that will turn you in a more secure person. Try to be unhappy and pessimistic walking around like this. It's simply impossible.

You can talk about something all day long, you can dream about something all day long, you can think about something all day long, but nothing will happen **UNLESS you initiate a real change of behavior and take ACTION.**

One last thing: BE PATIENT. Change takes time.

20

WRITE DOWN YOUR GOALS
AND ACHIEVE THEM

Brian Tracy says that 'People with clear, written goals accomplish far more in a shorter period of time than people without them can ever imagine.' This might sound a bit far-fetched - until you start taking it seriously and try it out. The results will be amazing. They will change your life.

If you start writing down your goals, you will become a lot more productive and probably more successful than ever. You'll be more relaxed and feel a lot less stress. And don't take ours or Brian Tracy's word for it. These are scientifically proven facts. And the best thing is that you don't even have to reach all your goals to have a great life, but more on that later.

Almost everybody makes the mistake of overestimating what they can do in a month, and underestimating what they can do in a year. They set very ambitious goals that they want to reach in a short time, and after a month they give up because they don't seem to be making any progress.

How can we change this? Well for starters, we can set a series of smaller and more achievable goals. If you stick with this method of smaller goals, these can add up to something enormous over the course of a year.

We want to convince you to make setting goals a way of life, both in your personal life, and your professional life or business. The simple act of setting goals for yourself and reflecting on them will launch you into the 5% of people who are goal-setters, and you will have an advantage over the other 95%. Yes, a whopping 95% of people don't have goals.

People who set goals are generally more successful, and the main reason for this is that goals give us focus. Concentrating on a goal provides us with the internal and external resources that are necessary to achieve it. Countless studies prove that having goals improves our performance, our well-being, and even our ability to recover from setbacks (precisely because we concentrate on the future).

When you set a goal, you are declaring that you believe that you will achieve something, which then turns into a self-fulfilling prophecy. When we declare something, when we say it out loud, it's more likely to become a reality—only talking about it is not enough, though.

So what do goals have to do with our happiness? Well, goals understood correctly lead us to happiness. But—here it comes—it's not the achievement of the goal that will make you happy. It's having a goal that will make you happy. Achieving the goal will only give you a temporary high that will pass, and you'll go back to your base level of happiness and strive for the next goal. Having a goal gives you direction and purpose, which will help you continue when others give up. You need a goal for future direction and purpose so that you can enjoy the present more.

YOUR goals must be aligned with YOUR interests and passions, rather than imposed on you by outside parties—not by your parents, not by your friends, spouse, neighbors, society, not even by your proper sense of loyalty or obligation. They need to be meaningful to you—'Want-tos,' not 'have-tos.'

Talking about goals without talking about values is

impossible. Not moral or ethical values, but values in the sense of what's fueling you, what motivates you. Knowing your values is very important. If your goals are aligned with your values, you'll meet a lot less resistance on the way. If there is a big difference between the life you live and your values, you continuously feel tension and suffer. Once you figure out what your values are, you'll be able to understand yourself and your actions better.

You can discover your values by asking yourself the following questions over and over again:

- 'Is this something I really want do or achieve, or is it something I have to achieve?'
- 'What are my goals?'
- 'What am I really interested in?'
- 'What am I passionate about?'
- 'Which moments bring me joy?'
- 'When do I truly feel like I'm being myself?'
- 'What is really important in my life?'

Like we said, ask your self these simple questions over and over again. The answers aren't that easy, which is why we usually don't ask them, and prefer to watch cat videos on Facebook.

Sometimes the answers are not what you want to hear.

Sometimes they are not pleasant. Sometimes you might even have to swim against the current, making decisions which are not the most popular ones. Answering these questions can be scary, and you'll need courage, but they are essential questions. They are the questions that can change everything. They are the questions that make everything worthwhile.

Having goals is not enough. Writing down your goals will make the difference. Writing down shows your commitment to your goals, and will move you to take action. When you write down your goals, you declare to your mind that out of the 50000 to 60000 thoughts your have every day, THESE written ones are the most important ones.

Writing down your goals will also help you to focus on the activities that bring you closer to your goals, and to take better decisions. When you take a look at your written goals every day, you compel yourself to take action, and it will help you to prioritize your actions for the day since you will be asking yourself questions like 'At this moment, is doing what I'm doing bringing me closer to my goals?'

Self-sabotage and self-deception are also a lot more difficult when your goals are written down, as opposed to only having them in your head.

It's vital that you set clear goals, such as 'I'll increase sales by 5% until December 2019', or 'I'll run 5 km four times a week.' If you have big goals, divide them into small achievable action steps, and make a list of all the steps you have to take to get there. Then calculate how much time you'll need to complete each step, and don't forget to set deadlines, both for each action-step and the main goal.

Don't worry too much if you don't reach your goal by the exact date that you set. This is just a way to concentrate on the goal and create a sense of urgency. We would go so far as to predict that if you set various goals in various areas of your life like career, recreation, health, finance, romance, etc., and reach only half of them in the next 365 days, it will still have been the best year of your life! If you don't believe us, try it!

In the exercise at the end of this chapter, we would like you to write down what you would like your life to look like in 10 years. When you do so, we want you to write down what it is that you WANT (even if it seems to be impossible), not what you think is possible. So THINK BIG. Your imagination has no limits. Your answers are the direction you are giving your life. Create a clear vision of your goals in your mind. See yourself as if you had already achieved your goal. How does it feel? What does it look like? How does it sound? How does it smell?

It's also crucial that while going after your goals, you reward yourself for the effort - not only for the results. Celebrate every small win, every milestone, every action step taken. Self-punishment is not allowed. Remind yourself that you are already a lot further than a week or a month ago, and a whole lot further than the 95% of the population that don't even have goals.

And above all remember: the most important thing about goals is not achieving them. Achieving them won't make you happier or unhappier. The most important thing is that goals energize us, motivate us, liberate us, and therefore are a means to an end.

Having goals won't save you from failure on the way to success, nor from difficulties, insecurities, or disappointments, since these are normal and inevitable. Meaningful goals will help you overcome these setbacks and keep you going and persisting on your way towards success and happiness.

Exercise:

1) What do you want your life to look like in 10 years? There are no limits! Think big!

2 What do you need to have achieved in 5 years' time

in order to be closer to your goal in 10 years?

3) What do you need to have achieved in 1 year in order to be closer to your goal in 5 years?

4) What do you need to have achieved in 3 months in order to be closer to your 1-year goal?

5) What are the things that can you do NOW to reach your 3-month goal?

Action Steps:
Write down at least three things and TAKE ACTION!

21

THE POWER OF YOUR WORDS

Be careful with your words. Not only when you communicate with others, but also—or even more—when you talk to yourself. Yes, we talk to ourselves continuously, eight to twelve hours a day. Yes, that voice in your head, the one that just asked you, 'voice? What voice?'

Don't underestimate the immense power of your words. With time, you will become what you are telling yourself all day, every day. The words that you use to describe your experiences become your experiences. It's just like the repeated suggestion of a hypnotist.

The most important part is what comes after the two little words I AM. How do you describe yourself? I'm lazy.

I'm bad. I'm useless. I'm weak. I'm stupid. I'm a failure. If you talk to yourself like this, you're doing a lot of damage because you will end up believing it.

Changing the way you talk to yourself will change your life. Get used to being kinder to yourself. You should talk to yourself as if you were your best friend, yet most of us speak to ourselves in a way that would make our fiercest enemy cringe—or happy, for that matter.

Start by saying nice things to yourselves, like 'I'm intelligent,' 'I'm handsome,' 'I'm beautiful,' 'I'm healthy,' 'I'm full of energy,' or 'I'm unstoppable.' Be patient if you don't believe yourself at first, and keep going.

Whatever you say to yourself, you'll see a reflection of it in your world. Your inner dialogue is so important because it has a massive impact on your self-esteem. Once again, be very careful with the way you describe yourself and remember this chapter the next time you catch yourself saying, 'I'm a disaster,' 'I'll never be able to do this,' or 'I'm so tired' (the more you tell yourself how tired you are, the more tired you will get).

We become our conversations. The way you communicate with yourself changes the way you think about yourself, which changes the way you feel about yourself, which changes the way you act, which ultimately influences your results and how others perceive you.

Scientists have been able to prove that words can alter the mindset of a person, which in turn changes their achievements and results. Words affect our performance and also how we affect the mindset of others. In one experiment, the cleaning personnel of various hotels lost weight and lowered their cholesterol simply because they were told that the work they do had the same effects as exercising. In another experiment, when researchers reminded elderly people that in general memory gets worse with age, the participants did worse on memory tests than others of the same age that weren't reminded of this fact.

Keep the conversation with yourself positive by telling yourself things like 'I want to achieve success,' 'God, I am good,' and 'I'm a lot of fun to be around,' and—one last warning—speak to yourself positively, because somehow your subconscious mind doesn't 'understand' the little word 'NO.'

Don't think of a pink elephant! See, I'm sure you just saw a pink elephant in your mind.

So what do you think happens when you say 'I don't want to be overweight.' Exactly. Our brain will understand 'I want to be overweight,' and get the juices going so that you get hungry even though you just ate. The same goes for

'I don't want to be like my father or mother.' If you're saying it often that's precisely how you are going to turn out.

Before we come to the end of this chapter, remember that words, and above all the questions you ask yourself, have a significant impact on your reality.

Say 'How can I do this?' instead of 'I can't do this.' If you ask 'how?' your brain will start searching for the answer and eventually will find it.

You really can change your life by changing your language, changing your conversations with yourself and others, positively talking to yourself and others, and starting to ask different, positive questions.

Why wait? Start now!

22

NEVER EVER GIVE UP

There are many recipes for success. Some work, and some don't. The safest bet is one that comes from Thomas Alva Edison, one of the greatest inventors in history, with over 1200 patents: 'The most certain way to succeed is always to try just one more time.'

Don't give up. Perseverance and persistence are the most important character traits when you set out to achieve happiness and success. They are even more important than intelligence, talent, and strategy. (Talent is totally overrated.) Never ever give up. Never.

When things don't go as planned, persist. Many times the only difference between success and failure lies in persevering, in trying one more time. If you read the biographies of the most successful individuals in the world, you'll see that all successful people have two characteristics in common: patience and perseverance.

It's highly probable—and inevitable—that before you achieve success, there will be some—or many—obstacles along the way. The important thing is to see those defeats as temporary and not as a permanent failure. When you fall, get up and keep going, change plans, change your strategy, and try again. If the new plan doesn't work either, change it again and again until it works. But be careful. Persisting doesn't mean persisting in a plan that does not work. It means persisting in achieving in your goal. If you are obsessed with your goal, you will find a way to achieve it. You might need double the time, but you will achieve it.

As we mentioned before, the only difference between people that reach their goals and people that don't is that the vast majority of people give up too early; they lack patience and persistence in coming up with new plans.

Persistence can be learned and cultivated. Your persistence is developed through the setbacks you encounter. The obstacles, the things that don't happen for you, the misfortunes. Each time you meet one of these situations along the way, you cultivate persistence. If you fall, get up, wipe off the dust and keep advancing towards your goal.

The habit of persistence is built the following way:

1. Have a clear goal and the burning desire to achieve it.
2. Make a clearly defined plan, and put it in practice with daily action steps.
3. Be immune to all negative and discouraging influences.
4. Have a support system of one or more people who encourage you to move forward with your actions and to pursue your goals.

Another thing that scares us to death is failure! What if it does not work, and if it goes wrong, and if, and if, and if. So what? No problem at all!

Behind the stories of the greatest successes, there are also stories of significant failures. Michael Jordan, for example, was eliminated from his high school basketball team. Steven Spielberg was rejected three times from film school. Walt Disney was fired by the editor of a newspaper for lack of ideas and imagination. J. K. Rowling, the creator of the multibillion-dollar Harry Potter franchise, was a divorced single mother who was unemployed while writing her first book. Stephen King, one of the most successful writers on the planet, was rejected 30 times by publishers.

Oprah Winfrey, one of the most successful women on TV, and today a multimillionaire, was fired from her job as a TV presenter for being considered 'not suitable for television.' And the list goes on. Behind every success story, there is the story of one or more failures.

Failure is part of life, part of success, and even part of happiness. What would your life be like without the fear of failure? Or without the fear of what others will think if your project doesn't work? It would be great, right? And undoubtedly a whole lot happier.

So let's talk about failure and debunk this myth once and for all. I (Marc) will start: In the last four years, I have had more failures than ever. I was rejected (and even ignored) by a lot of publishers. Some editorial managers laughed right in my face. I still haven't reached my goal to be interviewed in Catalonia's most widely read newspaper. I've had nothing but rejection from them. I was also ignored by more than 30 literary agents, many of my so-called 'friends' turned their back on me and walked away, and my marriage fell apart.

This is just to name a few. I've probably forgotten another dozen of failures, but you know what? These last years have also been by far the happiest and most successful years of my life. One of my books was published by Spain's biggest and most prestigious publishing house, and my books have been translated and published by renowned publishers in Korea, Japan, Russia, Indonesia, Thailand, China, and India, and I now have more agents looking out for me than an NFL player.

And yes, I've been interviewed in Catalonia's second most read newspaper, as well as in podcasts that have a lot more impact.

'Failure' is inevitable, and if you want to be successful you might have to fail many times. However, I have some good news: even though failure and rejection always hurt a bit, like everything else, it hurts a bit less each time.

I hope this testimonial helps you overcome your fear of failure because this bloody fear is the number-one dream killer.

So, one more time: THERE IS NO FAILURE. Okay? Take comfort in Napoleon Hill's words: 'Every adversity, every failure, every heartache carries with it the seed of an equal or greater benefit.'

We hope you can see failure in this light from now on. As a learning experience, an experience that is necessary for your growth. A fact that gives you information and motivation. Nothing else.

Accept your mistakes as feedback and learn from them.

Remember how you learned to walk: falling and getting up, over and over again. You didn't fall once and say, 'I will never learn this, and so I will not try anymore. Dad, carry me everywhere.'

NOW is the time to change your attitude towards failure. There is no failure, or better said, every 'failure' is an opportunity that allows you to learn and grow.

Remember:
Success is the result of right decisions.
Right decisions are the result of experience.
Experience is the result of wrong decisions.

YOUR TURN:
Have you had any failures in recent years?
What have you learned from the experience?
What positive things did you get out of it?

Another big fear we have is the fear of rejection. How many things do we not ask for, merely for fear of being rejected? Let's go. Let's do away with another myth. To achieve success and happiness in life, you will have to learn to manage rejection because just like failure, it is an inevitable part of life.

Also, rejection is not really the problem; the problem

is the internal dialogue that you begin after being rejected: 'I knew I couldn't do it. I know I'm not good enough. Dad (or Mom) was right: I will never achieve anything in life.'

Believe us. The most successful people are not very different from you. They only know better how to handle rejection. Now that's good news, isn't it? You can assume that on the way to your goals you probably will have to face rejection many times. No worries, it happens to the best of us. Just one thing: don't give up!

The most important thing is not to take rejection personally (we know this is easier said than done). It is only a person's opinion who at this moment does not want to go out with you, does not want to buy your product, does not want to read your manuscript, etc. Also, absolutely NOTHING changes in your life. If you ask someone out and he or she does not want to go out with you, in reality nothing has really changed. He or she was not going out with you before, and he or she is not going out with you now. Your situation is the same. The important thing is to continue! The goal of the most successful sellers is to hear the word 'NO' 100 times a day, because they know that if they hear 100 noes, there will also be some yeses. It's a simple numbers game! So get ready to be rejected many

times on your way to success. The secret is to not give up!
When someone tells you, 'No, thank you,' think: 'NEXT,
please.'

23

THE MOST IMPORTANT TOOL

This tool might change your life: a morning ritual. It is said that the most important hour of your day is the sum of the 30 minutes after waking up and the 30 minutes before going to sleep. That's when your subconscious mind is most permeable and receptive. Everything you do in that time has a multiplier effect on your day. Unfortunately, during that important time, most people think of everything they hate about their day, job, and life, or how things could go wrong.

The way you start your day has a significant impact on how the rest of the day unfolds. If you start off on the wrong foot, it's quite likely that it's going to get worse. Luckily it also works the other way around: if you wake up expecting that everything is going to go fine, it probably will—the only difference is how you interpret the situations that you encounter throughout the day.

This is why starting your day well is so important. There are countless book about what the 'Miracle Morning' (to cite the book by the same name by Hal Elrod) can do for you. Just give it some time. Like everything else, this will not change your life in one day. You have to start by training your attitude and then practice, practice, practice until it works.

How would your life change if instead of starting the day stressed from the minute you wake up, you started it by getting up half an hour or an hour earlier? If instead of hurrying and gulping down your breakfast (or even eating it on the way to work), you got up half an hour earlier and had thirty minutes of 'me-time'?

A short morning ritual that includes a five-to-ten-minute meditation can change your life in extraordinary ways. Here are a few activities that the world's most successful people do during their morning ritual. Try some of them out.

- Think positively: Today will be a great day because I will make it so.

- For five minutes, recall and reflect on things that you are grateful for in your life—and write them down.
- Five to ten minutes of silence or meditation.
- Imagine how today everything you do will turn out fine.
- Watch a sunrise.
- Go running or for a walk.
- Write into your journal and plan your day.

That's it. Committing to doing any of these (or parts of them) consistently for a number of weeks will change everything.

You want even more? Great attitude! If you're going to multiply the effect of the morning ritual, establish an evening ritual in the last half an hour of your day before going to sleep. It has the same importance. The things you do in the half an hour before going to sleep will resonate in your subconscious mind while you sleep. Here are some suggestions as to what you can do:

- Write in your journal again.
- Reflect on your day. What did you do great? What could you have done better?
- Plan tomorrow today: What are the most important tasks you want to get done tomorrow?

- Make your to-do list for the next day.
- Visualize your ideal day or life.
- Read something inspiring. Blog entries, articles, or some chapters of a book.
- Listen to music that inspires you and makes you happy.

I highly recommend you not watch the news or horror movies before going to bed, since they get you all worked up, and when you are about to fall asleep you are at your most receptive for suggestions. It's much more beneficial to listen to or watch positive material. It's also a good idea to put your phone away an hour before you go to bed. Studies show that you'll sleep much better.

Planning your day ahead and making a to-do list have enormous advantages and can save you a lot of time. It's like magic. It's like already working on the tasks that you have to do the next day in your sleep because they are already in your subconscious. You will notice that you'll work in a much more focused way the next day because you are already aware of your priorities.

There is more: getting up half an hour earlier every day you'll earn 182 and a half hours per year that you can invest in other activities. Even if you get up 15 minutes earlier, that's still 91 and a quarter hours!

That's two additional work weeks per year that you can put to use on what you love most.

There is exceptional energy in the early hours before sunrise. Starting your day this early has enormous benefits for your happiness and peace of mind. Many successful leaders were and are part of the early morning club, for example, Nelson Mandela, Mahatma Gandhi, and Barack Obama, as well as many others.

Getting up early is a habit, so give it some time. Don't give up if in the first two weeks you still feel tired after waking up early. Go out and spend some time in nature whenever possible. Watch a sunset or a sunrise. It's magical.

My favorite habit of the whole ritual is gratitude. It's the one thing I never skip. Be grateful for what you have every day, and you'll attract more things to be thankful for. Gratitude recharges you with energy and boosts your self-esteem, and it is directly related to physical and mental well-being. The 'attitude of gratitude' will lead you straight to happiness and is the best antidote to painful emotions like rage, envy, resentment, and sadness. Be grateful for what you have, for all the small things around you, and even for the things you don't have yet.

Start your day by being grateful for what you have—

instead of complaining about what you don't have. This will have an immediate effect on your life. Concentrate on the good things that you encounter every day, and you will start seeing them everywhere!

24

STOP HANGING OUT WITH TOXIC PEOPLE

I f you want to be happy, you have to be very careful about who you spend your time with. Stay away from the negativity of toxic people and add the positivity of people who support you in your life. Associate with people who help you grow as a person, avoid people who belittle your achievements, and get out of relationships that constantly hurt you.

What Jim Rohn said decades ago, that 'you are the average of the five people you spend the most time with,' has now been proven by science, so you'd better start to take it seriously. Emotions and attitudes are contagious.

Spend more time with the people who bring out the best in you, who motivate you, and who believe in you, because they are the springboard to motivate you and help you take the right course of action. On the other hand, spend less and less time with the people who drag you down, who exhaust you, drain your energy, and who act as brakes in the achievement of your goals in life. If you spend a lot of time with negative people, you might become a more negative and cynical person over time.

While you are at it, you can boot those who want to see you stuck, too. Stay away from people who always say, 'You can not do it,' from those who still blame others for everything that doesn't work in their lives, from those who complain all the time—you already know who I'm talking about. Do not listen to their opinions, and trust your own inner voice. It will be challenging to prosper, grow, and be happy if the people around you do everything they can to convince you that it will be difficult. Even just spending less time with them or taking a temporary break can improve your self-esteem quite a bit, thanks to the decrease of negative input.

Unfortunately, many times the energy vampires will be people you are close to, including family members or your innermost circle of friendships. This makes things a bit complicated, and I won't be the one to tell you that you ought to turn your back on them. What I am saying is that you would do well to seriously consider staying away from people who damage your self-esteem, self-confidence, and your happiness. Spending less time with them or going longer and longer periods without seeing them can be a start, and can seriously improve your well-being due to the reduction of negativity. But those decisions are totally up to you.

Sometimes it also happens that while you work on your personal development and growth, negative people stop seeing you as interesting because you no longer serve their purposes. To them, you're weird now. They need someone to share their complaints and their negativity with, and if you don't do that anymore, they will look for somebody else. They'll probably tell you that you've changed, that you're not like you used to be, and they might even tell you that you've gone completely crazy. If they tell you the latter, do not get nervous. Maybe it's a good sign. Most of the successful people I have talked to have this in common when they pursue their dream: many people think they have gone completely crazy and turn their backs on them.

If spending less time with toxic people or taking a

timeout from them doesn't work, then you should seriously consider not seeing them at all, although this is a private decision that only you can make.

Only one thing: life is far too short to spend your time with people who do not treat you well and with respect. Release them from your life and make new friends. Say goodbye to all the people and relationships that rob you of your energy.

Choose your relationships wisely, especially romantic ones. Much of your future success will depend on it. Remember that you're the average of the five people you spend the most time with. But you know what? This is even more true of the one person who is around you the longest. Our relationships are the number-one predictor of long-term happiness. The only thing that all extremely happy people have in common is good interpersonal relationships. But it also works the other way around. Being surrounded by negative people can seriously damage your self-esteem and self-confidence.

Get away from relationships that no longer nurture you. Get away from people who do not value you. Get away from negative people. We will repeat it, just in case: life is too short to spend it in bad relationships with people who detract from your happiness. Yes, it often takes more courage to get out of a bad relationship than to maintain it, but you can do it.

Sometimes, it is better to be alone than to be in bad company. Do not let lonliness lead you into a relationship, because there is nothing worse than being alone in a relationship. There is a good chance that your best relationship will come when you are truly okay with yourself. It's funny. When you no longer need a relationship to be happy, that's when you'll find a great relationship. Until then, work on the relationship with yourself, and be a great friend. Spend time with people who support and value you. Less is often more. Also, in the relationship and friendship department, choose quality over quantity. Have a few high-quality relationships instead of many superficial ones.

When it comes to the ONE relationship, Neil Pasricha, author of 'The Happiness Equation,' really drove an idea home for me. He makes the significant point in his book of how important it is to choose a happy partner, because, as we have mentioned, the person with whom you are in a relationship affects your happiness tremendously. Pasricha invites us to examine our romantic relationships with our partner or spouse, and examine how much of the time we are happy together, how often we are unhappy together, and how often one of us is happy while the other is not. These are fundamental questions, and you must be completely honest with yourself.

For example, if you are happy 80% of the time and your partner is happy 80% of the time, both of you will be happy together 64% of the time. 64% of your time together, both of you will be smiling, loving and happy. Those are the good days. Life is fun. Life is good. It also means that you are in a lousy mood together 4% of your time together (20% multiplied by 20% is 4%). Those are the bad days, the difficult days, the fights, the struggles. These are part of all relationships, and are normal. They will help you grow. This means that in 32% of your time together one of you is happy and one is not. That's a third of your time together. One-third of your time together, the mood of one person influences the other. The positive person will pull the negative person up, or the negative person will pull the positive person down.

So now comes the tricky part: Let's look at other numbers—people who have lived with a not-so-happy partner may recognize this. If you are happy 80% of the time and your partner is happy 40% of the time, then you are happy together 32% of the time, unhappy together 12% of the time, but suddenly 56% of your it time can go both ways. More than half the time you are pulling your partner up, or they are dragging you down. Careful now, you entered into this relationship being happy 80% of the time! It is very tiring and requires a lot of energy to encourage and cheer somebody up all the time. Finding a partner with your level of happiness or higher is essential. Is your partner adding to your happiness or wearing you out?

25

LISTEN TO PEOPLE, REALLY

emingway said it a long time ago: 'When people
talk, listen completely. Most people never listen.'
And boy, was he right. One of the most essential
tools of any coach, salesman, or leader (and definitely one
of the most important lessons in my coaching training) is
the ability and the skill to listen profoundly to the person
you are talking to, a.k.a 'Active listening.'

Listening profoundly means listening to the person in
front of you while giving them your full attention. It means
silencing the little voice in your head that already knows
the solution for the other person thirty seconds after they
begin to speak. It means NOT rehearsing in your mind
what you are going to answer once the other person stops

talking. Many people do not listen to understand, but only to answer! They are just waiting for their counterpart to pause to start talking.

Do not interrupt. Listen until the person has finished. If you want to give advice, ask for permission. Most of the time, the person you're talking to will find his or her own solution - if you let them finish talking. Test it out! It is possible to take your conversations and your relationships to a whole new level if people feel that you are really listening to them. People are not used to the fact that someone really listens to them, and even less in these times when everyone just wants to show how smart and cool they are. Listen well! It will be a 'competitive' advantage for you. You listen. You will make people happy, and that will make you happy.

Another extremely important thing for your happiness is the little word 'NO'. When you speak, say 'no' a lot! Once you learn to say 'no' to people, commitments, things, or at work, your happiness will skyrocket.

There will be people in your life who will want to convince you to do things even if you do not want to do them, and sometimes because you want to please everyone, you will say yes, even if your inner voice shouts 'NOOOOOO!' Be careful. Saying 'yes' when we want to say 'no' really does hurts our self-esteem, and the usual result is that later we feel a little sad or even angry because once again, we gave in even when we had something better to do. Learning to say 'no' will improve your life a great deal. You will become more YOU, because every time you say 'yes' when you mean 'no', you lose a bit of yourself and your self-esteem is hit.

When you decide that a 'yes' is a 'yes' and a 'no' is a 'no', you will feel much better. This means fewer commitments and, although saying 'no' to your friends and family is difficult at first, the benefits of it are great.

Don't others say 'no' to you all the time? Still, most of the time you do not get mad at them, do you? Well, you can start saying 'no' too, and no one is going to get angry. Let's assume that the people who really like and love you are not going to get upset. That's why saying 'no' is also an excellent way to filter out toxic and false people. While these individuals might make something of a scene, your real friends will understand you and will still like you even if you tell them 'no' from time to time. They may even love you more because you are being more authentic.

In your work life, the impact of saying 'no' can be even greater and improve your situation a lot. In fact, you will gain a lot of time. If you don't say 'no', you will be the most loved person in the office. You will also feel overwhelmed, working extra hours when the others go home because you will be doing the work that no one else wants to do.

The most successful people say 'no' very often. Be sure to say 'no' without feeling guilty. You can explain to the person in question that it's nothing personal against them, but that it's for your own well-being. You can still do your colleagues a favor, but only if you have enough time and decide to do it.

Selfish? Yes! But don't forget who is the most important person in your life. YOU are the most important person in your life. You have to be happy. Only when you are happy can you infect others with this happiness. You can always buy some time and say 'maybe' at first, until you come to a final decision. Life becomes much easier when you start saying 'no'!

26

SPEND TIME WITH YOUR FAMILY

A multitude of studies proves that the number-one predictor of your happiness is the quality of your social relationships, both at home with your loved ones and at work. Science has shown that relationships make us happier, more productive, committed, energetic, and resilient, and that when we have a network of people we can count on, we recover faster from setbacks. Thanks to relationships we achieve more, and we have a greater sense of purpose. Relationships are a natural necessity. No one can survive or prosper without relationships. Relationships make a real difference. The fact of being happy and sharing this happiness improves relationships. Similarly, when you go through hardships and difficulties, relationships help you overcome them. Certainly, the most important relationship is your relationship with your nearest and dearest. Family is not only important—it's everything!

Walt Disney once said: 'A man should never neglect his family for business.' Still, how many people do you know who work 60 hours a week and claim to do it for their family? Of course, we all have to earn money to support ourselves and our families, but if you really want to do something fabulous for your family, spend more time with them. Science has even proven that in the long run, it's the best thing you can do for your performance at work. Besides, one of the greatest regrets of the dying is 'I should have spent more time with my family and less time in the office.' It is not a coincidence that everyone says it. Wake up! Do not become one of them and start saving time for your family NOW!

It's a little sad that I even have to mention this because it should be clear, but when I interview leaders and executives, most of the time it appears that they simply 'can't' spend a lot of time with their families.

When you are with your family, do everyone a favor and be 100% present. Switch off your phone. Stop thinking about work and give them 100% of yourself. Many years ago, on a vacation in the Florida Keys, I saw an absurd situation. A family was taking a tourist walk, with the father running ahead, making a business phone call (I could tell because he was speaking very loudly), while the wife and daughter followed him with a sad look on their faces, which was totally understandable. It was even Sunday! It seemed like something out of a comic, and yet it was very real and sad to watch.

When I say 100%, I mean phones OFF and away. It's okay if for an hour or two you do not answer the phone (except if you are a surgeon or emergency personnel on call—then do not listen to me). When you are with your family, the phone goes in the drawer.

In 2016 a Common Sense study measured that 50% of teenagers and 27% of parents admitted to being addicted to their mobile. And while 77% of parents said they feel that their children do not pay attention to them and are distracted by their devices, 48% of children said the same thing about their parents. Other studies show that we look at our mobile phones up to 150 times a day. Another study by Przybylski and Weinstein found that the mere presence of a mobile in a face-to-face conversation reduces the feeling of being close and connected, and therefore reduces the trust and quality of the relationship, even if the phone is not being used. So when you are with your family, for at at least one hour, put the phone away.

Your phone is for YOUR convenience, not for the convenience of those who call you. Give yourself the freedom to continue what you are doing, and let the call to go to voicemail. They will call back. If it is something very important, the caller will not give up, and will probably call five times in three minutes.

Wake up! Value your family and your friends. They are your constant source of love and mutual support, which increases your self-esteem and your self-confidence.

27

BELIEVE IT UNTIL YOU BECOME IT

Act 'as if'! Act as if you had already achieved your goal. Act as if you already had that quality of life, lifestyle, work, etc. Do as William James said, 'If you want a quality, act as if you already had it.' This really works. What William James said over 100 years ago, today has been scientifically proven. If you want to have more confidence in yourself, act like a self-confident person. Speak like a self-confident person, walk like a self-confident person, adopt the physical posture of a self-confident person. Act 'as if' you already had a certain strength, character quality, etc. In neurolinguistic programming and coaching, this is called 'modeling.' An excellent way to be happier is to observe and copy happy people. Start acting 'as if' and see what happens. Fake it until you become it!

Ask yourself the following questions: What quality do you want? How would you act if you already had this quality?

Do you want to test right now how your posture influences your well-being, and how changing your posture also changes your mind? Let's get to it then: When you feel sad and depressed, you usually look at the ground, walk with your shoulders down, and adopt the posture of a sad person, right? Next time, try the following: stand up, raise your shoulders up, push out your chest, hold your head up high—even exaggerate a bit by looking up.

How do you feel? Come on, smile a little, even if you have to force it at first. Raise your shoulders a little more, keep your head a little higher, look up a little higher. I bet you are already feeling much better, aren't you? It's impossible to feel sad walking like that, isn't it?

A 2009 study by Brion, Petty, and Wagner found that people who were sitting straight had more confidence in themselves than people who were sitting slumped over.

I highly recommend you watch the fantastic TED talk by Amy Cuddy called 'Your body language shapes who you are,' about the research she did together with Dana Carney at Harvard University. The study showed that adopting 'power poses' for 2 minutes increased testosterone by 20 percent (which increases confidence) and decreased cortisol by 25 percent (which reduces stress).

This is great before a presentation, meeting, competition, or important interview. Adopt the position of a self-confident person for two minutes. Put your hands on your hips and spread your feet (think of the cartoon 'Wonder Woman'), or lean back on a chair and extend your arms. Hold your posture for at least two minutes, and see what happens!

Spend 20 minutes NOW to see the TED talk by Amy Cuddy!

28

YOUR BEST INVESTMENT

What will your best investment ever be? Any investment in yourself! You are number-one in your life. As the saying goes, 'You can change the way people treat you by changing the way you treat yourself.' So treat yourself very, very well. For starters, make a list of 15 things you can do to take care of yourself, and do one of them every two days for the next four weeks. They can be small things, like reading a good book, going to the movies, getting a massage, going on a weekend getaway, watching a sunrise, sitting by the water, etc. This exercise is truly miraculous! Once you start to treat yourself very, very well, it will work miracles for your self-confidence and your self-esteem. Start doing it NOW!

Another very important thing is to continuously work on your personal and professional growth, and to invest in your training and personal development. Derek Bok says it clearly: 'If you think education is expensive, try ignorance.'

Commit yourself to becoming the best person you can be, investing around 5-10% of your income in training, books, CDs and other forms of personal development.

One of the characteristics of the most successful people is that they always remain curious, eager to learn new things and to improve and reinvent themselves continuously. An interesting side effect of investing in your personal growth is that as you become a wiser person, you can also become more valuable to your company.

We live in a world full of possibilities. You can get the best books or online courses from the most reputable experts with a click, without ever leaving your house, or even your sofa. You can participate in training that improves your negotiation skills, time management, financial planning, and much more. In a course or workshop of two to four hours, you can learn powerful strategies or tools that will transform your life.

The best investment in myself that I ever made was hiring a coach at one time and a mentor at another, both of which were cases when I felt stuck. They helped me out of being stuck, find clarity about what I really wanted in my life, and about the next steps I had to take. The funny thing is that on both occasions I recovered my investment within a few months, and then multiplied it.

You can also start with less expensive methods: by reading or listening to an audiobook, or taking a course. I have made it a habit to read at least one book per week, buy a new class every two months, and enroll in at least two seminars or training courses per year.

What are you going to do? Remember that small steps are also worthwhile!

Commit yourself to read x number of books per month, listening to y number of learning CDs, audiobooks, or podcasts per month, and to enroll in z training courses in the next 12 months. If you do, let me know how your life looks a year from now. I'm sure it will never be the same.

Be careful, though. Do not fall into the trap of thinking that you always need to take one more course or read one more book before starting your dream project. It is very, very important that you apply what you learn. Many people take one course after another and never apply what they have learned. They always think that they need one more course to become perfect and then use their knowledge. This, my friend, is a colossal mistake and is called sabotaging yourself. Take action and apply what you have learned right away. Go!

29

HOW TO DEAL WITH PROBLEMS

Have you ever noticed that most people spend more time and energy looking for excuses or for the people responsible for their problems than really solving them? What a loss of energy, and what a strange phenomenon. It would be so much easier and more efficient to concentrate on the solutions to the problems. These people could save a lot of time and energy, let alone the anxiety and discomfort they go through.

A big step towards your happiness is to face your problems head-on and solve them. If you don't, they will follow you anyway. Have you noticed that your problems repeat themselves again and again until you learn something and are ready to move on? Have you seen that you find the same set of problems in multiple romantic relationships until you stop to solve them? What if, for example, you changed jobs because of problems with a colleague that you didn't face? Later on, in another job, you would find the same challenge again, simply with a different person. I'm afraid that if you do not learn something from the situation and solve the problem once and for all, this pattern could continue indefinitely.

This always happened to me in relationships. There were always the same situations, the same problems, until one day I confronted the problems and I asked myself, 'What the hell am I doing?' It's not the other person—we have to look at ourselves and see what we can change to solve the problem once and for all.

If you overcome your fears, face the problem, and you solve it, you will feel much better. In addition, you will realize that it was much less painful to face the problem and solve it, than to go through the whole process of dancing around it. And most importantly, you will realize that the solutions to your problems are not 'out there,' but rather they are inside of you. All this will serve as a point of reference for the resolution of your next problems. If you have done it once, the second time will be easier, and the third time even more so.

So stop a moment here. Make a list of all your problems, examine them, look for patterns (do the same things happen to you again and again?), and start to solve them little by little.

The following questions can help you:

How can I be different?

What can I do differently?

What can I do to solve the problem?

And as if we didn't have enough with our own problems, we often worry about other people's problems. Don't get me wrong. Empathy is a great virtue, but I think that first we should literally clean our own house before we start cleaning the neighbor's house, or even worse, giving him advice on how he ought to clean his house, while ours is still a disaster.

The Dalai Lama gives us quick and short directions to deal with problems. I use it in most cases: 'If a problem can be fixed, if the situation is such that something can be done about it, then there is no need to worry. If it cannot be fixed, then worrying does not help. There is no benefit at all in worrying.'

Many people are always worried. They worry about

things that happened in the past, that they can not change (which is a waste of time and energy); things in the future over which they have no influence (which is even more of a waste of time and energy); or about the economy, wars, and politics, over which they have no control (a still greater waste of time and energy).

Have you noticed that most of the catastrophes that worried you throughout your life never actually happened? And those that did happen turned out to be much less horrifying in reality than in your imagination? Mark Twain was right when he said, 'I've had a lot of worries in my life, most of which never happened.'

It doesn't matter how much you worry. Worrying will not change the past or the future! Also, worrying, in general, does not improve things. On the contrary, it drags you down and makes you miss the present moment. Do you grasp the loss of time and energy that worrying is causing you, or would you like me to give you another example?

Here it comes, in the form of a simple exercise that I learned from one of Robin Sharma's books:

1. Make a list of your worries and problems
2. Which ones are related to the past? Mark them with a cross.

3. Which ones are related to the future? Mark them with a cross.

4. Which ones are out of your control? Mark them with a cross.

5. Strike out or erase all the worries and problems that you have written in points 2 to 4.

6. What are the problems you can really do something about (the ones not crossed out)?

Generally, after crossing out all the worries about the past, the future and those that are out of your control, you will probably be left with 5 to 10% that really deserve your attention.

By identifying your problems and releasing those to which you can't do anything about, or that only drain you of your energy, I dare say that you can eliminate 90 to 95% of the worries that have been torturing you so much.

If not, try a more philosophical approach: do you have many problems? Congratulations! You have many opportunities to grow because a problem is always an opportunity to grow, since you can learn from it. Some say that our problems are our best friends, and others see them as blessings. Do you see how a problem changes when you change your perspective?

A small change in perception or a small change of words can make a huge difference. If you use the word 'challenges' instead of 'problems,' it might be very beneficial for you.

It might not be a bad idea to change now, because one thing is for sure: you will always have problems. Isn't life facing one problem (or challenge) after another? What will make all the difference in your life is how you confront them and how you learn from them!

Once you start learning from your problems, life gets much better. Don't say, 'Why is this happening to me?' Say, 'What can I learn from this?' Look back and have a look at the problems you have had in your life. Didn't each of them have something positive?

Perhaps a loss in business saved you from an even more significant loss, because you learned from the situation. In difficult times, it can be very beneficial to adopt the belief that life, or God, or the universe only puts a problem in front of you if you are able to solve it.

30

MORE HAPPINESS HABITS

Wow! We have already reached the last chapter. Here we have the final boost of happiness. And yes, a truly happy ending. Here we'll tell you more about the best simple and easy-to-practice habits that can add a lot of happiness to your life.

1. Smile more!

Smile! Even if you do not feel like it! The act of smiling improves the quality of your life, your health, and your relationships. If you don't do it yet, start consciously smiling NOW. Laughter and smiling are very good for your health! Science has shown that laughing or smiling a lot every day improves your mental state and your creativity, and better yet, you even live longer. Smiling can change your stress response in difficult situations by, for instance, slowing down your heart rate and decreasing stress levels. Your smile sends a signal to the brain that things are going well even when you do not feel happy. (You still shouldn't ignore your emotions, but it's a little help).

If you have no reason to smile, hold a pen or chopstick between your teeth. This simulates a smile and produces the same effects because it stimulates the same muscles in your face as a smile. This means that when you smile, your whole body sends the message 'Life is great' to the world.

Smiling makes us feel good and even diminishes pain. It also reduces blood pressure and stimulates the functioning of our immune system. Smiling makes us happy—just try to be pessimistic while you smile, and you'll see. So smile a lot. Watch half an hour of comedy each day and laugh yourself to the point of tears. It is the best medicine.

All of this can help give you a little boost of happiness at times. It doesn't mean you should fake feeling good or smile all the time when life isn't going so well. It's important to be honest to yourself about your emotions.

2. Listen to your favorite music—every day!

One of the easiest ways to feel happy instantly is to listen to your favorite music. Make a playlist with your favorite songs of all time and listen to them, dance, and sing. You may feel a bit silly at first, but doing this every day will be very, very beneficial to you. So make this list NOW.

3. A random act of kindness every day

If you give kindness to others, it usually comes back to you, so use this in your favor. Innumerable studies show that happiness grows when you help other people. They say that spending money does not buy happiness, but scientists have found otherwise: spending money on other people or experiences makes you happier. You can make the world a little better by being kind to a stranger every day.

Offer your seat on the train, hold the door open for someone, pay the toll for the car that is behind you, store someone's hand luggage on your next flight, be generous with you smile, etc. Get creative. Remember that 'what goes around, comes around.'

If you perform a selfless act every day, after a while, you will realize that people will perform selfless acts for you.

The hard part is, of course, not expecting them to do so.

Praise people sincerely, treat people nicely, thank them genuinely. Once you acquire the habit of acts of kindness, doing well by others will begin to be the same as feeling good. Improving the world begins with you. Start today and do at least ONE random act of kindness every day. Make an impact on the lives of other people in a positive and meaningful way, and your happiness will skyrocket.

4. Celebrate your victories and have something that brings you joy every day

On the road to happiness, it is very important for you to be aware of your progress. Stop from time to time and celebrate your victories both the small ones and the big ones. Celebrate that you are better than you were last week. Do not let your little victories go unnoticed. Reward yourself. Buy yourself something you always wanted, go to the movies, or do anything else that makes you feel good. If you have learned new habits and have noticed a significant improvement, maybe you can reward yourself with a short trip. You have earned it. What will you reward yourself with for your progress so far? Are you going to have a spa day or a nice dinner? Are you going to go for a walk?

It is important to have something to look forward to. Do not let routine and boredom enter silently into your life. Create things that make you happy after a hard day's work, instead of ending up in front of the television every night.

Celebrate something: the fact that you have work, your family, or simply life itself! Call a friend you have not called in a long time, or better yet, if you live in the same city, take him or her out to lunch.

5. Be grateful for what you have

If you asked me about the most important ingredient of my success, the ingredient that took me from being jobless to being a best-selling author, I would answer one thing: gratitude.

The power of gratitude is amazing. Once you start to adopt an attitude of gratitude, you will notice the benefits in a matter of weeks. It is scientifically proven that people who practice gratitude become happier, more optimistic and more sociable. They sleep better, have fewer headaches, more energy and show more emotional intelligence. They are also less likely to suffer from depression, and they feel less anxious. Gratitude is also a proven antidote to envy, anger, and resentment.

Gratitude reprograms your brain to see more of the positive things that surround you. You will see more opportunities, and you will see doors open for you, where before there was not even a door. Make gratitude a daily habit. It's magical. The more grateful you are for what you have, the more things to be thankful for will enter your life. Be grateful for what you have and even for the things you do not have yet.

I know that when you are going through a difficult time, it can be hard to be grateful. But the truth is that there is always something to be grateful for. You can start with simple things like being alive, breathing, your talents, your friends, your family, or nature. Start with small things.

When I was out of work, I was grateful for having a coffee in the sun, for sleeping well, and for having friends. Instead of starting your day complaining about what you don't have or fearing what is to come, start it by saying 'thank you' for what you do have. Concentrate on everything that is going well for you.

When will you start to write down those three things that you are thankful for each day? Write them by hand and—this is very important—feel the gratitude with all your body and soul.

6. Exercise

We all know how important exercise is, but most of us just don't do it. The best excuse is always: 'I don't have time.'

We have made a list for you of some reasons, to see if you change your mind:

1. Exercising will keep you healthy.
2. Exercising will help you lose weight, which will improve your health.
3. Exercising will make you feel better, and you will have a lot of energy.
4. Once the kilos begin to melt, it's very possible that your self-esteem rises.
5. After exercising you will sleep better.
6. Exercising significantly reduces stress.
7. Exercising makes you happier.
8. Exercising can reduce the symptoms of depression.
9. Exercising reduces the risk of diabetes, osteoporosis, high cholesterol, etc.
10. Exercising decreases the risk of premature death.
11. Exercising improves memory.

Are you going to exercise? We have good news! Walking also counts as exercise. If you walk 30 to 60 minutes every day, then you are exercising.

One last thing: do not force yourself to exercise. Try to enjoy it. Find a recreational activity that suits you and that you like to do, such as swimming. As we have already mentioned, even walking an hour a day can make a difference.

7. Write in your journal

One last habit of happiness before we say goodbye. It has been scientifically proven that having a diary and reflecting on your days adds to your happiness. If you spend a few minutes at the end of your day to take a look at what you did well, to get some perspective, to relive the happy moments, and write down everything in your journal, you will reap many benefits in the form of more happiness and more personal development.

It also has the positive side effect that, just before sleeping, your mind will be concentrating on positive things, which will have a beneficial impact on your sleep and on your subconscious mind. In these key moments before sleep, your attention will be focused on the positive things of the day and gratitude, instead of the things that did not work and that would probably keep you awake.

It's as simple as answering the following questions every night before bedtime and writing them down in your journal:

- What am I grateful for today? (Write 3 to 5 items.)
- What three things have made me happy today?
- What three things have I done exceptionally well today?
- How could I have made today even better?
- What is my most important goal for tomorrow?

The words may not flow immediately when you start this exercise. Don't worry, that's normal. Like anything else, writing in your journal will improve with practice. If you are blocked and can not think of anything, just wait five more minutes. Write what comes to mind without thinking much, and do not judge. Do not worry about your style or mistakes. Just write! Do this every day for a month, and observe the changes that take place.

EPILOGUE

By Manuel Villa

A few months before we started writing this book, Neale Donald Walsh, the famous author of Conversations with God, told us after a talk of more than two hours in Madrid, 'This afternoon Mooji (another of the great spiritual gurus of our time) will be on stage and will tell you something very similar to what I have told you, with less than half of my words and intellectual effort. The key is that we all agree on what is important. After that, everyone must go their own way and try for themselves.'

Marc and I also completely agree on the essential things. While he puts more emphasis on habits, enthusiasm, and happiness, I may concentrate more on resilience and the necessary complicity of empathy. Nonetheless, the idea is the same, because our perspectives are simply two sides of the same coin.

Life is not black and white, but rather it is comprised of a thousand and one shades and nuances, and the grace, the secret, is in the contrast, the games played by light and shadows. As in the breath and the heartbeat, our vital processes of inhaling and exhaling, the systole and diastole, tension and distension, and the feelings of joy and sadness, courage and fear, anger and calm, fullness and emptiness— all these pairs come together to make up an inseparable whole. It is the mind, or the ego, that strives to separate, to distinguish, to fragment, to judge, and to catalogue: this yes, not that. And when this happens, we only want to take away the pleasure, and in the face of pain or suffering, we flee in terror, losing with it all the enjoyment of living intensely.

The subtitle of this book, *From Suffering to Happiness*, does not presume to suggest a linear path of undaunted progress, but a harmonious dance between pains and glories, in which ultimately the latter dominate. Because meditation and useful thought in the here and now transform the mere pleasure with results into enjoyment of the process, opportunities are created where before there were adversities, we find learning where before we saw errors, and we find compassion where before we stumbled over suffering.

That said, as we have seen in this book, we should not fall into overly simplistic visions. Everything is very simple if we do not complicate it, but the fact is that we complicate it, so there is work to be done.

Thoughts and emotions cannot be controlled. Leaving neurotic thoughts aside is not an easy task. And emotions follow thoughts. The novelty that we have discovered and worked on together throughout these pages is that we can indeed better manage those same thoughts and emotions if we put all our focus and energy on our attention and our conviction.

This process has its stages: a change of attitudes, a change of beliefs (going from limiting beliefs to other stimulating and empowering ones), a review of strengths and values, and finally, a commitment of repeated action, hence the talk about habits. We already know that first we create our habits, and then our habits create us. Such is that on this journey, we build ourselves through the power of habit, or rather, we rediscover our essence.

In any case, you first have to open the door to change. Attitudes are key in this regard. Without true will, there is no start. We will never make a real turning point without having defeated those 'four horsemen of the Apocalypse'; let's once and for all get rid of idealized perfectionism ('It will not work out well'), senseless arrogance ('I do not need to hear or learn anything else'), bitter doubt ('I do not know if it's worth trying, so I'll do it half-heartedly'), and the eternal wait ('Now is not the time, maybe later').

Only with firm conviction can we better ourselves. It takes energy to be able to overcome inertia or inherited and very consolidated patterns. Do not let yourself be overwhelmed by them ('I can not handle it,' 'I will not make it,' 'I'll start, but I'll fail').

To reach that winning determination, this absolute and unshakable faith in ourselves, we need a great deal of clarity regarding our values, our strengths, and our weaknesses. We have to know what we really want, and not just what we would like. Putting it in writing helps.

Without proper inspection and maintenance, our car will break down on the first hill. Without knowing our priorities, every tree seems like a shelter and every road a shortcut, and so we spend our lives looking for comfort without recognizing that, if we do not know where we are going, any and all paths lead us on, perhaps to our downfall.

Let's be honest, let's stop making excuses, attempts and 'tolerances,' let's take control of our lives, recognize our responsibilities, grasp our potential, and enjoy what this moment offers us. That is, without a doubt, true happiness.

It has been a pleasure to walk with you. Now go and enjoy your journey.

You can contact us here:

manuel.villa@mindfulzen.es

marc@marcreklau.com